T0209738

RULE
YOUR LIFE

How to heal from your past and present
traumas and start living again

Jenica Lee

BALBOA.
PRESS

A DIVISION OF HAY HOUSE

Copyright © 2019 Jenica Lee.

All rights reserved. No part of this book may be used or reproduced by any means, graphic, electronic, or mechanical, including photocopying, recording, taping or by any information storage retrieval system without the written permission of the author except in the case of brief quotations embodied in critical articles and reviews.

The information, ideas, and suggestions in this book are not intended as a substitute for professional medical advice. Before following any suggestions contained in this book, you should consult your personal physician. Neither the author nor the publisher shall be liable or responsible for any loss or damage allegedly arising as a consequence of your use or application of any information or suggestions in this book.

Balboa Press books may be ordered through booksellers or by contacting:

Balboa Press
A Division of Hay House
1663 Liberty Drive
Bloomington, IN 47403
www.balboapress.com
1 (877) 407-4847

Because of the dynamic nature of the Internet, any web addresses or links contained in this book may have changed since publication and may no longer be valid. The views expressed in this work are solely those of the author and do not necessarily reflect the views of the publisher, and the publisher hereby disclaims any responsibility for them.

The author of this book does not dispense medical advice or prescribe the use of any technique as a form of treatment for physical, emotional, or medical problems without the advice of a physician, either directly or indirectly. The intent of the author is only to offer information of a general nature to help you in your quest for emotional and spiritual well-being. In the event you use any of the information in this book for yourself, which is your constitutional right, the author and the publisher assume no responsibility for your actions.

Any people depicted in stock imagery provided by Getty Images are models, and such images are being used for illustrative purposes only.
Certain stock imagery © Getty Images.

Print information available on the last page.

ISBN: 978-1-9822-2181-2 (sc)
ISBN: 978-1-9822-2183-6 (hc)
ISBN: 978-1-9822-2182-9 (e)

Library of Congress Control Number: 2019901627

Balboa Press rev. date: 03/08/2019

CONTENTS

DEDICATION

This book is dedicated to my CHILDREN and to YOU, the reader. Throughout my own healing process, I have learned to LOVE myself again. Now, I can give my children the best of me by teaching them to LOVE and how to receive LOVE. I have become their example of how to LOVE oneself, LOVE each other and LOVE life. It's a joy to LOVE them. I'm following my life's purpose by being the best mother I can be and to share God's LOVE through words to help others.

GOD IS THE WIND

Here I go, walking through life fighting against the cold blowing wind as I'm dragging my emotional baggage. The struggle is real, I feel my face burning. The howling of the wind is so loud I can't hear myself think. I have no choice but to push through, this is all I know. My mind, body and soul are exhausted. My destination is unknown. I have no sense of direction, I'm lost. Some of you might relate to this scenario. My life was that scenario, now I know it was by choice. This book is in your hands for a reason, your desire for change have directed you here. We all experience a different type of journey but eventually we end up on the same path. This path takes you to the power of God, Jesus and the Holy Spirit. Jesus brings salvation, forgiveness, healing, love, peace, hope, joy and eternal life. God healed my life and he can heal yours too. God's power can heal your past and present traumas. Some of you may have had a good childhood but experienced trauma as an adult. Some of you may have the little girl or boy in you feeling trapped because of your trauma. I understand that as human beings we question, why? Why did this have to happen to me? Especially when things are done to us from a young age - when we are helpless and vulnerable. The memories of any trauma stay with you throughout life. You may think you can ignore or avoid the pain by choosing sex, drugs, and/or alcohol. How long do you live your counted days living in misery? God is waiting for you to stop fighting change and allow him to help you become free of those memories. Take back what's rightfully yours. Peace, love, freedom, healing and joy awaits. Right now, seize this moment and become self-aware because you are important. Decide to want more out of life and get ready to Rule Your Life. Then God will give you steps to take so you can receive your healings. You have one life to live, so start living again. You are the son or daughter of the

Almighty God, fix your crown. Stand up straight and know that you are blessed already. Get excited about the day and allow yourself to become truly fulfilled. God loves you.

Years ago, I would find books to skim through searching for quick solutions, always wanting an answer to, "why am I feeling this way?" These feelings meant different things at different times. There were times I felt lost, angry, hopeless, unhappy, the list goes on. At the finale of each book, the author would give me my "aha moment." I would feel better for just a few days and back to my miserable place. Now, I'm the author and I would like to say this to you, "figuring yourself out is a process!" There is no quick solution, healing from your past and present traumas takes time. Just like a cut on your finger, there's a process of healing happening. Cleaning the wound, wrapping the wound and making sure it does not return. Making the decision that the time is now will open doors for the healings to take place in your life. In this book, I give you my life story. My timeline is mainly focused on the parts that broke me. It's the broken part of me, that got victory at the end. Discovering God helped me turn my back against the wind, to allow the wind to carry me to the path of healing and of transformation. God is everywhere, he is everywhere and because of him I am a living testimony. If I can do it, so can you. If you're ready to heal from your past and present traumas, faith in God is required. Be patient, take notes, allow your faith to grow and be willing to change the direction you're walking in, so you may achieve victory as well.

We all have a unique story to tell, this is mine. As a child, I experienced childhood traumas and throughout my childhood I believed that life was rough. Trauma is a disturbing experience that causes sorrow, pain and stress. My parents divorced because of my dad's infidelity and drug-use. Growing up as a fatherless daughter, created unnecessary struggles for me. The absence of his love, and not having a relationship with him had caused me to feel unworthy. When I did see my dad, he was busy doing nothing. My mom was busy too, but she was working to support her four children. She worked a lot to make sure our needs were always met. Nonetheless, hearing multitude of complaints about making ends meet from my mom and stepdad was stressful. Financial problems are a stressor for any age. Kids shouldn't hear about adult problems. My heart was broken, my mind was stressed and to add to that - trusting males was hard for me. I hid secrets for decades about being molested. I lived my life with many burdens but holding on to the hidden secrets was the heaviest to carry. There was a lack of communication from my parents, which hindered my growth on how to express myself verbally. Every child needs undivided attention. Giving them a moment to express how they feel when asked, "how are you doing?" "what's your high and low of the day?" I've learned that you must push through adversity and never give up. My view on life had a negative outlook, but I had an inner feeling that things would be alright.

That inner feeling never left me. I was born and raised in the Midwest, with nice summers and cold-depressing winters. At the age of six, the first man that I loved abandon me emotionally - my father. After my parents divorce, I would see him on some weekends hoping to get his attention. He didn't love me the way I needed him to and that made me sad. There was no real connection between us, he would just greet me and feed me. Having a broken heart had kept me in a yearning state for his love, affection and attention. As I got older, I found out he was a heroin addict. My grandparents on the other hand were my everything. They did what my dad should've done. Every weekend, my brother and I were picked

up by them. Even if the weather was below zero or a rain storm, they were there on time. I lived with my mom and stepdad full time. My mom was a superhero to me; our home would smell like Pine-Sol, there would be food cooking on the stove and at the same time she was putting clean clothes away. She liked jamming to Spanish music and her mood was mostly upbeat. As great as she was, the financial struggles were never ending. Hearing my mom say, "we can't afford that" or "I don't have enough money" was a part of my upbringing. Despite that, I also remember many times my parents coming home after work with grocery bags, we never went to bed hungry that's for sure. They did provide for us, but as a kid hearing their stresses about needing more money gave me anxiety. Sometimes, I would worry about them not having enough and I would stop myself from asking for extra things. While they worked, I was the world's best babysitter for my three brothers. I'm the oldest sibling, the leader of the pack. We had fun times, many stories that we still talk about today. Being young and having to carry that responsibility, shaped my character to become selfless. Unfortunately, not everyone is selfless.

I've experienced inappropriate touching by selfish male family members and a male doctor. Different body parts have been touched, I can remember each time like it was yesterday. Seeing a penis at five is disturbing. I remember thinking, "what is that?" Molestation comes in different forms, it can be body contact, or no touching involved. My innocence was taken away from me because of their improper behavior. It was difficult for me to speak up about my violations because I was confused, and I didn't know how to express myself. Part of that confusion also stemmed from being taught to respect and listen to my elders, which made my confusion even worst. Everyone knew me as a shy and sensitive child. I would cry often because it was a way to get attention and to cope. Being naïve wasn't the problem, the problem was the lack of supervision from the adult(s) that were watching me. I would like to bring awareness to you or to someone you know. We naturally trust family, friends, teachers and doctors but they can be the first to break that trust. I say this to you from experience, "watch your children and talk to your children!" As I entered adulthood, I buried my feelings of shame and all the sadness that came with it. I chose not to talk about my childhood traumas with anybody. At that time, I didn't know it was considered trauma. What I did know was that forgetting about it seemed to be the easiest route. I focused on my independency. Graduating college had given me some fulfillment. After this accomplishment though, my heart was set on finding love and I wanted attention from a man. I looked for love in the wrong places and settled for losers. I fell in love with a guy named Sammy, and like my father he was a heroin addict. We decided to have a baby and get married because we loved each other. Within a few years the love started to fade away. We consistently argued, he verbally abused me, he was jobless, and he was a jail bird. I admit it, I had no standards which put me in a horrible marriage that in turn created adult trauma in my life. My daughter would be right in the middle of all the chaos. Being in an unstable relationship caused us to separate a lot. I couldn't deal with him anymore, I divorced him.

Following the divorce, my daughter and I left Illinois and moved to Florida. We were ready to start our new life in a tropical environment. Giving her stability and keeping her safe was a must. She liked her new school and was doing well. It was just her and I for a while. I started to date a guy named Frank. Frank is seven years younger than me. Eventually, we fell in love and got married. I had a son and a daughter from my husband. Most of the time, Frank was the breadwinner and his

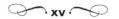

goal was to have a happy family. He knew I had been through a lot. At first, being happy wasn't easy for me, the inner victim wouldn't allow me to be. I would nitpick at everything he did, I had a control issue. To me, he couldn't do anything right. We would argue, and my raging anger would unleash. I commonly released my frustration by yelling loud, it was the only way I knew how to be heard. My kids would be home and I knew the arguing had to stop. Smoking marijuana was my solution, it helped me stay calm. The kids were always taken care of and I would have the house spotless and like my mother, smelling like Pine-Sol. However, spending quality time with them was something I needed to work on. I was inconsistent with doing fun activities with them. I also needed more communication with my young children. I knew that I didn't get quality time while growing up, but I told myself I must figure out how to break the cycle of the lack of bonding. I struggled with living in the moment and I worked on correcting that. Reading books on that subject helped me become more present and active.

Internally I wasn't present with myself. Putting a fake smile to the world, pretending I was great while my insides were like a volcano ready to erupt. I hid my feelings and problems so well that everyone assumed I was ok. My family and friends depended on me. I have a natural helper spirit, I often volunteered to be the go-to person for favors and advice. But their dependency on me became unbearable. I was consumed by their problems and being emotionally attached to it led me to constant complaining. My emotions were suffocating me. The blame game made it easier to push everyone away. As time went by, I broke up friendships, I wouldn't answer the phone and I disappeared from some family. Seclusion was needed, so I could figure myself out. Questioning myself, "why am I miserable?" I was miserable because I was a mess, I never processed my traumas. Childhood traumas are experienced in different ways but can have similar emotional & psychological symptoms. The symptoms I experienced at different stages in my life were: denial, confusion, anxiety, anger, sadness, shame, depression and seclusion. As an adult, all those symptoms carried over. Plus, I added more trauma to my life by making bad decisions. Not knowing my self-worth contributed to my problems. Having a negative mindset didn't help either. I told myself I had to resolve everything, while at the same time I was thinking life is hell. The stress was wearing me down. I started to think, "what is wrong with me? Why do I feel unhappy?" The heaviness in my heart made it hard to breathe. A realization overcame me, that I had to take responsibility for my life and to start loving myself again. I wept and thought, "I just want to be happy!"

As an adult the urge for happiness followed but also, I was "feeling stuck." I made up my mind and I knew it was time to heal my heart and get my mind right. Seeing a counselor was something I refused to do, that wasn't the route I wanted. I believed that God started to nudge me. Ignoring my conscience, left God with no choice but to shake up my world. God got my full attention when my son was diagnosed with a rare disease. Right before my eyes, I witnessed my son receive a miracle from God and my faith grew. I got on my knees and started to pray. I thanked God for saving my son's life. I knew I had to follow God and learn to trust him every day. My spiritual journey began and overcoming my past and present traumas became my mission, I was ready to Rule My Life. God's lead was vital for me, he knew what steps I needed to take. Listening to him was crucial. Following his way led me to Jesus and the Holy Spirit. In my healing process I was more than healed, I was awakened, and I learned about myself. My mind was

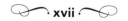

renewed and only then was I transformed, which prepared me to start living again.

I share my story, advice and God's wisdom in this book for you. I encourage you to become self-aware and I hope you're ready to Rule Your Life. You must act on a decision to change something about yourself or about a situation, for a more meaningful life. Allow your life traumas to take you on a spiritual journey. It's important to discover and recognize God's power. With faith, you can receive healing from your past and present traumas. Within your healing process you'll be awaken, able to learn about yourself, renew your mind, transform and start living again. You have a destiny to fulfill and you're in charge of creating a fulfilling next chapter for your life. Believe in God and believe in yourself for God loves you.

"I can do all things in him that strengtheneth me."
Philippians 4:13 (American Standard Version)

CHAPTER 1

THE SILENT CHILD

As I sit outside under a canopy listening to rain, thoughts are flowing from my mind to my fingertips. God's Holy Spirit inspired me to type direct messages from him to you, these messages are written in **Bold** font. I've also added Bible verses from the American Standard Version likewise written in **Bold** font. Everything written in Times New Roman font is from my memory, perception, opinion and advice. The character names were changed to protect the privacy of those depicted. My spiritual journey has led me to my beautiful God given purpose, which is to share God's love by helping others. In this book, I wrote in detail about my traumas and how I overcame everything. God gets the glory for my healings and for this book coming together. God wants you healed and to start living your life, how it was intended to be lived. He knows what you need, God is your guide and he is your answer. I believe that God is the creator of everything. God is the father, the son Jesus Christ and the Holy Spirit. The Holy Trinity is one God in three divine persons. It's God's will to save, heal and give you a new life but you must have faith. To have faith, it requires believing in God's power. His healing power will come through you in his timing. Understanding who God really is can happen with having a relationship with him through Jesus and following the Holy Spirit. Jesus died for our sins and rescued us from our own punishment. Jesus then resurrected to complete the work of our salvation. Jesus promised to send the Holy Spirit to be with us after his death and resurrection. Accepting Jesus Christ is the only way to have the Holy Spirit active in your life. The Holy Spirit is God's personal presence, his active force. The Holy Spirit is in God, in Jesus and if you invite him, he will be in you also. You have a human spirit that can connect and experience the Holy Spirit. The purpose of the Holy Spirit is to have a guiding system to follow, so you can live your best life.

No one is perfect; however, you can become a better person be it a better parent, friend, sibling, spouse - if you follow your heart. You may be relying solely on your mind and think you're doing your very best, but as humans falling short is inevitable. Living your life your way can cause pain to yourself and to others, especially your children. It's your choice on how you want to live. God gives you free will, you can decide if you want to follow your way or God's way. While God has many names, his power is unchanging; In the ASV bible version he is called Jehovah. If you need a better understanding of the verses you may look up a different version.

"And Jehovah God formed man of the dust of the ground, and breathed into his nostrils the breath of life; and man became a living soul." Genesis 2:7 (American Standard Version)

Humans have a body, spirit, soul and mind. "The dust of the ground" becomes the physical body. "The breath of life" is the human spirit. "Became a living soul" refers to the soul, which is a person's will and their mind. Your body is housing your soul. Your spirit is the deepest part of your being, it is a receiver. The purpose of receiving my spirit is to have a relationship with me. The soul is who you are, you are eternal and always present. Your ego takes control over your soul, if you allow it. Your soul is connected to heaven, it is your final home. Living a purpose filled life is the ultimate plan for you. Follow your inner desires to do more, feel more. To love and to be

loved. You are beloved by me. I give you peace,
health and love my child.

Going back, way back into time, I was born in the seventies.
A unique little thing I was, I had brown hair with blonde tips, a
porcupine hair style, and big blue eyes. I recall my grandfather
boasting to me about a group of strangers who were staring at me
through the nursery hospital window, giving him compliments.
He was a proud grandpa! My parents were young, they had me
at only sixteen-years-old. They had to figure it out and raise me.
So they chose to marry, and we moved into our first apartment.
My first imprinted memory is at three-years-old, hearing loud
music playing. Pink Floyd – "Another Brick in The Wall" is the
song I remember. That song on replay, played over and over. I
was crying in a dark room standing in my crib. Recently, my
aunt confirmed that memory for me. She said, "your dad was
watching you and your mom was at work…I lived upstairs and
heard you crying from one of my bedrooms." She continued,
"I came down to tell him that you were crying and to turn off
the music." She recalled voicing to him, "pay attention to her!"
As I grew up, each time I heard that song, I would stand still
almost frozen. The song always took me back to that moment,
experiencing a feeling of helplessness. Eventually with time, I
got over it. I knew he was young and now I can visualize him
back then rockin' to that song. Through healing, I can now
laugh each time I hear it.

A parent's duty is to love, secure, provide and teach their
child how to become a productive adult. The secure part
requires keeping a child's innocence protected because it helps
shape that child's future. At the age of five-years-old, I was
not being watched properly. I say this because a male family
member named Diego was able to touch me, with his penis.

We were in a closed room by ourselves. Diego said to me, "pull your pants down." I told him, "no." Yet he proceeded and pulled his pants down. I was looking at this thing (his penis) it looked like an elephant – the closest thing my mind as a five-year-old child could associate a penis to. Diego connived and said, "if you want more horsey back rides, you need to pull your pants down." I started to pull them down slowly, I was unsure. He pulled my underwear down as I was holding them tightly, never letting go. He then progressed to touch my vagina with his penis. I stepped back, getting away from him and pulled up my underwear and pants quickly. Diego questioned, "where are you going?" I ran so fast out of that room and hid behind a chair in the dining room. A lot of thoughts came to my mind. Being absolutely puzzled about what happened made it hard for me to tell anyone. I knew I had made a mistake by pulling my pants down and I didn't want to get into trouble for that. Listening to my elder, as I was taught, just didn't seem right this time. I stood hiding, I was scared. I knew I could never ask him for another horsey back ride. The doorbell finally rang, it was my mom. She was there to pick me up, so I got up to wait by the front door. As soon as I was outside with her, I wiped what had just happened right out of my mind.

Other recollections remained in my mind. Post me being born, my dad had two women pregnant at the same time. His wife (my mother) and his new girlfriend were three months apart. My mom had a boy and the girlfriend had a girl. I remember one day finding a diaper in our car, under the seat. I told my mom, "here mom, I found a diaper." She looked to my dad and said, "this isn't the brand we use." They had an argument, one of many. One evening, my mom and aunt drove to confront my dad and the other woman. I was in the car and witnessed everything. They shook and shook my dad's car, to make the alarm go off. My dad and the girlfriend came outside from an apartment building. I remember thinking, "why is my dad with that other lady?" My parents started to argue, and my aunt was beating up the girlfriend. The fight and argument finally ended and so we left. On this occasion like others, my mom forgave my dad. But those times of forgiving him would eventually end for her. I remember at six-years-old, my mom telling me to say goodbye to my dad. My mom knew my dad was still in a relationship with his other babies' mother. He didn't know we were leaving him, he thought I was going to school. I wanted to tell him my mom's plan, but I didn't I just said, "bye" and hugged him. At that moment, my heart was broken. I walked away thinking, "why did he have another family?" "Does he still love me?" "Would I ever see him again?" The sadness I felt had made me cry but I thought at least I said bye. I had a lot of uncertain feelings about him but with my mom and brother I was certain about being safe. She would always tell me she loved me and I felt the love from her, she was always gentle and caring. We went out of town for about a month.

After the month, arriving back to my hometown was exciting for me, I wanted to see my family. We started our life over after our return, living near my new school. My mom's new boyfriend moved in with us. I was shy and observed him, he seemed nice. One day, my dad found out we were back in town and confronted my mom, a family feud occurred. We were in the car with my moms' parents. Out of nowhere, I saw my dad and my dad's parents right next to us. My mom instructed me, "don't open the car door to anyone!" Everyone stepped out of their cars. My mom was arguing with my dad, my grandfathers each had their fist up circling like boxers and my grandmothers were pinching each other. My grandmother from my dad's side told me, "open the car door." I told her, "no."

I was scared, confused and started to cry as I was holding my baby brother thinking to myself, "why is everyone fighting? I miss everyone." The arguing eventually ended, and we drove off. My mom was upset. I wanted to tell her that I missed my dad. I had questions too but didn't say anything. I found out later that my mom's boyfriend was not just her boyfriend but also my dad's cousin. The day of the family feud, my dad was confronting my mom for taking us out of town and for being with his cousin. It took over a year for my parents' divorce to become finalized. My mom was obviously done with him, but my eight-year-old self wasn't. Life moved on and my mom was having another boy with my new stepdad. We moved to different apartments causing me to transfer schools. I was timid and transferring to a new school was terrifying. It didn't help that some students would make fun of my shoes because they weren't name brand. Leaving me out of the recess games because I didn't fit in. Asking my mom for more shoes led me nowhere. I was told by her, "you have shoes already maybe next month you can get some." The next month came and I asked for name brand shoes. I got a big fat "no!", I hated being poor.

During the weekends, I would visit my grandparents from my dad's side. We would sing, laugh, go out to eat and watch baseball on television. Great times with them, I felt the love. My grandfather would always make me feel special. On some weekends, I would see my dad. At this point in his life, he had five kids and three step kids. He would gather all eight of us and take us to a park. After the park, my dad would feed us and take us to our grandparents' house. The time would go by so fast and I never got any special time with him. I spent a lot of time outside with my siblings and step siblings. I remember often running away screaming "the church people are coming!" They were very persistent about attending church. While my family was Catholic, we didn't go to church regularly only for special events like a wedding or a baptism. At the age of ten, sad news came my way. My dad was arrested and was fighting a case for selling drugs. I had overheard that he was doing drugs too. All his kids were there for his sentencing hearing. We all cried as they handcuffed him and took him away. I felt crushed again, each time I wanted him he was unavailable. Yet driving far away, getting searched by guards and waiting hours just to be with him for a short period of time was worth it to me. We barely talked because the adults took up most of the time, but I was always looking forward to the next visit. I felt as if I was doing his four-year sentence with him. I would write to him and I would get excited when he wrote back. The letters meant everything to me, he promised me the world. My excitement from my fathers' letters didn't trickle to how I felt about my appearance. And so unfortunately, my excitement didn't last for too long because my appearance had changed dramatically. My vision went bad overnight. My teeth needed serious straightening. I had glasses and braces for a few years, which had me feeling like an ugly duckling. Some family and kids from school made it a point to tell me their opinion about how I looked. I had cheap eyeglass frames from being on welfare. I didn't know how to defend myself and just took all the hurtful comments. They made me feel like something was wrong with me. My feelings were hurt, and I cried in silence. Bullying is not okay!

As I became older, I was subjected to more sexual violations. At one time I was playing with my dolls and a male family member named Carlos started to hump my leg like a dog. An adult was near and saw what was happening and removed him away from me. I never seen him again. I became curious, wanting to know, why did he rub himself on my leg? The situation was never addressed to me by an adult, so I thought it wasn't a big deal. Another violation occurred when I was about twelve-years-old, my pediatrician was making sexual sounds as I bent to touch my toes during a physical examination. I stood up and he was behind me, squeezing my shoulders and then touching my breast. I felt so uncomfortable and wiggled my way out. He advised the physical was over. My mom was in the next room, I didn't tell her because I felt ashamed about it. The next time I was sick I convinced my mom to go to our previous doctor. Touching my breast happened at a different time again and was done by a male family member named Eric. He was standing behind me, acting like he was giving me a hug as he was touching my breast. I remember thinking, "why are men touching me?" I recall I dropped to the floor, so he could release the hug. The look he had on his face was different, he frightened me. I thought he was going to hurt me because he said, "you know your mom is not here, right?" I felt relieved when he walked away from me. The encounter made me feel fearful and I didn't want to experience that anymore. I got brave and I was ready to tell my mom everything that had ever happened. When I saw her, my heart was beating out of my chest. The subjects that we regularly talked about were school, food, and the weather. I just didn't know how to tell her that I had been touched. I left her side without telling her wishing she had asked me, "Is everything ok?" I was ready to say "no!" But she didn't ask and that night, I cried myself to sleep.

Pretending that I was ok was how I learned to live. I turned to things that made me happy, like listening to music and dancing. Summer breaks were the best. Every summer, I was excited to have our family vacation. My mom and stepdad took us camping, we would drive to Wisconsin Dells. We would go swimming, bike riding and sometimes the famous Noah's Ark

Water Park. Being on a budget meant eating sandwiches and hotdogs. Sometimes, she would surprise us with fast food and made sure to tell us, "I can't afford this all the time." She seemed to be stressed out, as she would count her money that in turn would stress me out. I wish I could've helped her. I told myself to be happy and I knew she was trying her best. One school year when school first started, we had our first babysitter. My mom worked second shift, and we would just sit on the sitter's couch for hours. I had an idea to take me out of my misery and help my mom, I asked my mom if I could stay home and babysit. She knew I was responsible and mature enough to do it. I started babysitting at thirteen, right before my baby brother was born. I took great care of all of them, especially the newborn when he was born. Helping my mom out made me feel good. I knew she could spend the babysitting money on other things plus I had the comfort of being home. Before work she would make dinner. I made sure to be in the kitchen with her observing and asking questions on how to cook. That became my quality time with her. Her food was delicious by the way.

I was fourteen-years-old and finally my dad was out of prison. Seeing him at his home and hugging him was the best feeling. He had made a lot of promises when we wrote to each other. One evening, my dad called me outside and I went running. I was happy, finally our moment together. He asked me, "can you ask grandpa for ten dollars? Tell him you're hungry and I will take you to a burger spot." I told him, "I ate not too long ago." He fessed up and said, "I owe my friend some money and I don't want to ask grandpa for it." I folded and just said, "Okay." I sat next to my grandpa and asked him, "can I have ten dollars for a cheeseburger meal?" He exclaimed, "What! Is this money for your dad?" lying I replied, "no." He insisted, "Are you sure?" again I lied and said, "yes." He gave me the ten dollars and stared right into my soul. I was extremely nervous but at this point any attention from my dad was worth the lie. My dad and I left in the car, we entered an abandoned looking neighborhood. It was dark out and he said, "I will be right back, stay in the car." At that moment, I was convinced he was back on drugs. We were in a drug-infested area, it was always on the news. On the way back, we passed a restaurant. I told my dad, "I don't want to go back empty handed, can I get a soda?" He said, "I don't have any money." desperate I said, "can you get a soda from the garbage?" My dad made a u-turn, the first trash can we saw happened to have a soda right on top of the trash can lid. We looked at each other making eye contact and had a moment. My dad told me, "I feel bad about this." When we got back, and I made sure that my grandpa saw the soda in my hand, then I tossed it. I avoided my dad the next weekend, I didn't want him using me for drug money. He never fulfilled his promises to me, I was disappointed in him.

Some time had passed, my body at this point had fully matured. Unfortunately for me, almost everywhere I went I saw men look at me with "pervert eyes". To me, pervert eyes is when the eye balls are bulging out of their eye sockets. Staring at me as if I was a piece of meat. I've learned to just walk away and move on with life. Not expressing myself on how I felt was something I had grew accustomed to. Years of bottling up my emotions had completely shut down communication between myself, my family and especially my dad. I wanted him to be my rescuer, my protector and just for once to focus on me. I knew he was a drug addict and he had problems, but I did exist, I was after all his daughter. I needed him. I don't even think he noticed that I stood away from him. At one point, I was angry. He was not my father anymore. With my brothers and sister, we would go back and forth saying, "he's not my dad he's your dad." None of us wanted to claim him. Holding in every sad emotion wasn't easy. I stood away from all men including my dad because I didn't trust them. All they did was hurt my feelings and make me feel unsafe. Being young, vulnerable, and hopeless had led my emotions to become deep sorrow in my heart.

At seventeen-years-old, I was depressed, I didn't have anyone to talk to. It seemed like quality time with my mom was impossible. She worked far away and would get home exhausted. Financially, things did get better for the family. My parents bought a ranch style house with a built-in swimming pool. Having more material stuff was nice but a lot was missing in my life. After school, I had a part-time job then home to babysit my brothers. Most of the time, I made dinner. Doing dishes was a must and I made sure they went to bed at a decent time. I felt like I was the third parent. I had a lot of responsibility and I just wanted to be appreciated. At one point in my teens the time had come to break up with my first boyfriend. He wasn't loving me the way I needed him to. It was a point in my life where wearing black and keeping my room as dark as I could was ideal. But depression didn't last too long because I was graduating high school. I was shocked to see my dad and uncle show up to my graduation. That was a special day, I had all my parents there. It was my time, time for me to become independent. Independence brewed and I questioned to myself, "what will make me happy?" I knew buying a car, starting college and finding a boyfriend was important to me. I was ready for some freedom. My cousin had a friend and he was the "man of my dreams." He was tall, handsome, and older than me. He was the first man to make me feel butterflies in my stomach. I was in LOVE. Seeing him on the weekends and receiving plenty of attention from him felt amazing. He was honest with me one day and said, "I made up my mind and I'm leaving town tomorrow for a new job." I thought to myself, "maybe he will stay if we have sex." I lost my virginity that night at nineteen. The next day, I was saddened because he still left. I never seen him again. To comfort myself, I came up with the excuse that I didn't want to be a twenty-year-old virgin anyway. I was able to focus on finishing my college degree, my perseverance had kicked in.

There were a lot of good times and great memories that I skipped over because if I had I'd be writing forever. I give my mom plenty of credit, she did the best she knew how because she loved me. My mom taught me nothing comes easy in life, and you must work hard to get what you want. Now, I have my own kids and I understand about making sacrifices. I will do anything for my kids. I'm grateful to have a wonderful mother like her. My grandparents tried to fill my broken heart with love. I'm grateful for them for trying their best but I still needed my dad. In this book, I shared the not so good stories, so whomever is reading this can feel like they're not alone. Relating to others is important. The adults in my life had failed to watch me properly. Failing to protect and secure me as a child against sexual predators. I am not protecting the males who violated me, I chose to change their identity due to legal reasons. I pray for every child in this world for protection against anything harmful. My innocence was taken from me, making each time harder and harder to communicate. A void that ran deep with hidden secrets that I chose to bury.

I want to bring awareness to you. We need to keep our eyes and ears on our little angels. Teaching them that their private areas are not to be touched by anyone is not enough. Having an open communication with them and asking questions can help them express themselves to you. Many benefits can come with communication, it can help save them from becoming a victim or stopping the victimization. If you have been victimized yourself, you can pray to God about it. He will help you heal, if you have faith. Our childhood sets up the direction on where our life will be headed. Giving your child a strong foundation to stand on is very important. It will bring confidence, self-worth and avoid the whole identity crisis. Since I didn't have a relationship with my dad, it caused me to stand on a broken foundation. I was abandoned emotionally and felt unwanted by him. My broken heart yearned for his love, attention and affection. Some kids have their parents at home and could still feel fatherless or motherless. Not having a relationship with your child means you're an absent parent. Breaking the cycle of having kids and not being there for them is my desire for all. I never talked about the molestations, and those experiences turned into shame. The shame was eating me up and I held it all in. My experiences made me a victim to the people who had violated me. The inner child in me was still silent, broken hearted and a victim. The young adult in me was ready to push through life thinking I was prepared.

CHAPTER 2

THE EGO LEADER

Understanding who you are and what you're capable of is essential for a long healthy life. Your soul has two parts, your will and your mind. Your will makes the decision to choose or to refuse. God has given you a fearless, empowering, and forgiving soul. Your ego is a part of the emotional side of your mind, intended to help deliver and explain information to you. It is your ally. If your soul doesn't want to lead, your ego will take control and make decisions for your life. That's when your ego wants to separate from God. Everything is about "I". You become consumed by your emotions, self-criticism and become focused on fear. Your ego turns from positive to negative and it's now your enemy. Your soul would never know what your ego is up to, it has its own mysterious plan. You might ask, "why would our soul give up leadership?" To put it in prospective, take the example of a child growing up in a dysfunctional environment, this causes pain to any child. The soul is forced to withdraw from its own life. The soul has no room for pain. However, through meditation or with prayer you could build a stronger relationship with your soul. The soul then becomes in charge again and the ego doesn't like that. There's a constant battle for control, the soul and ego will both need healing from God. Your ego becomes tamed once it's healed. Yet, you've created bad habits because of your ego, and it will feel like your ego never left. Stay focused on having a strong relationship with God and yourself.

> *"Trust in Jehovah with all thy heart, And lean not upon thine own understanding: In all thy ways acknowledge him, And he will direct thy paths." Proverbs 3:5-6 (American Standard Version)*

The purpose placed in your heart is a calling from Heaven. You have a destiny to fulfill. I do give you free will. Free will is - live your life how you desire to. Your soul is fragile, it will turn to your Ego for help. Living without Godly direction is your ego being in charge. Your ego will lead you by fear. Fear of getting hurt or rejected. Living a life of frustration. You can call on me for help and follow my Holy Spirit, I am your everything.

Entering my twenties, my childhood feelings were out of my mind. I focused on earning money with my full-time job. On weekends, I went out with different girlfriends (friends that were girls). Drinking and cruising around looking for guys was the thing to do. Looking for anyone who would give me attention. Hungry for love and thinking that promiscuity was ok. I was a magnet for attracting guys with drug problems. In fact, some of the choices I made had put me in dangerous situations. I wanted to be accepted by others, I wasn't being true to who I was. What it boiled down to was that all my wild actions were ways to cope with my trauma. I didn't even know I needed help. What I needed was to receive healing from God. The average person doesn't know they need help either. Coping in a negative manner is distracting oneself from how you feel. This can lead to drinking, drugs, sex, and/or depression. For some people, they may even cause self-inflicting pain. It's like adding dirt to your buried feelings. One night, I was being chased by a gang because I had the opposing male gang members in my car. I was driving like an egomaniac, thinking I was cool. I happened to drive into a dead-end street. As I was making a U-turn, I heard a loud crashing sound. Glass was everywhere, and my back window was busted. I drove even faster because I thought they shot at us. Getting back to our neighborhood was the goal and it was also time to drop off the fellas. Inspecting my car, I found a brick on the floor in the back. It was my car, and no one cared to help me pay for a new window. I decided to get away from that environment. Living on the edge gave me an adrenaline rush and my ego loved it. However, I couldn't afford that lifestyle. I started to make better decisions, at least that's what I thought.

On one snowy Sunday, I was cruising with my sister and friend. We met a guy his name was Sammy. He told me, "I want to get with you girl." I was giggling and feeling special because he picked me. We exchanged numbers. On our first date together, Sammy asked me to be his girlfriend. Of course, I said yes. While on our date, we picked up his friend Juan and drove to a familiar area. I knew that area because my dad drove me there once to buy drugs. I instantly asked, "why are we here?" He said, "my friend owes someone money." My next question was, "are you on heroin?" He admitted he did a little heroin on the weekends. He seemed like he had it together, so I stood with him. A month of dating had passed, and I found out I was pregnant. Sammy had another friend, he let us stay over his apartment because I was pregnant, and I was scared to go home. I became aware that his friends were all drug addicts and heroin dealers. I remember thinking, "I left my mom's house for this?" Everything was happening so fast, I was going to be a mother soon. Sammy got some money together, we got married and eventually got an apartment together. One day during my pregnancy, Sammy's friend Juan called Sammy and told him to stop by his job. Little did we know the police were watching all of us through the store cameras at Juan's job. As we were exiting the store the police stopped to question and search Sammy and me. I had baggies of Heroin in my pocket. I exclaimed, "that's not mine, I'm just holding it for someone!" I was handcuffed and driven to the women's jail. The female cop told me, "do you know that if you have your baby in jail that baby will be mine?" I told her, "I'm not due anytime soon." She retorted, "babies can come out whenever they want." I didn't reply. I swallowed my pride and stood quiet. Praying to God was the only thing to do, I was in fear. The food in jail was horrible, thick bologna and stale bread, Yuk! My mom bonded me out hours later.

In the fall, I gave birth to my daughter Camila. She was so perfect and looked like a porcelain doll. Her room was beautifully done, everything was pink and white. With the pending charges against me for the heroin possession, I decided to see a voodoo man to help me with my upcoming court case. He created a special candle for me to be turned on each time. And so, each time I went to court, I lit the candle for protection. Some time went by and I was found guilty of possession. I was given two years' probation. I believed at the time that the candle saved me. I was grateful that I was not given jail time and I was able to live my life with my husband and daughter. Sammy decided to become drug-free. He gained weight and looked younger. We loved each other. One month had passed and I noticed Sammy's behavior had changed. I knew he was back on drugs, I was disappointed in him. I suggested counseling because he needed it. He went but didn't finish the program. We argued a lot and he couldn't keep a job. Supporting his drug habit made me feel used. He was also verbally abusive, always calling me names, constantly being referred to as "bitch", "stupid bitch", or "dumb bitch". He would be mad because sometimes I would deny him money, or I would catch him in lies. My daughter was always present for the arguments. I noticed she started blinking differently. This blinking was a faster nervous almost twitch-like kind of blink. I knew that the arguments caused this change, so I kicked him out of the house. Her odd blinking stopped a few days later.

Sammy ended up getting arrested for something minor. It was summertime and I was ready to mingle. Us being separated gave me the justification to date whomever I wanted. I never got serious with anyone I was just being young and dumb. I would visit my family more often because I was happier. Fall season came, and Sammy was released from jail. We talked about making it work and he moved back in. He made promises that I hoped he was able to keep. Some time passed, and I believed he was on drugs again. He tried to convince me he was clean, still in doubt I would search his belongings and as my doubts were confirmed I would find his drugs. Whenever I found something, confronting him boosted my ego. My goal was to take control of his next step in hopes of "fixing" him. It became a challenge for me because I wanted to "fix" him. Counseling, detox, and/or going to church were the obvious solutions. Giving him trust and him failing each time made me feel as if I failed. We were living in a cycle of him being on drugs, denial of using drugs, losing his job, him back in jail, us separating, him off drugs and then released from jail. I lived through it and there was never any real progress. Living in a dysfunctional home and dealing with a drug addict came with a lot of bullshit. I just dealt with it and would even give him a daily allowance for his drugs. Thinking by doing this that I was in control of his intake, one bag a day was the agreement. He seemed to be "normal" and attempted to look for work. I was more like his mother holding his hand. I should've found someone that was able to live their own life in a productive way, but I never wanted to be alone. I settled because I didn't realize I was deserving of so much more. I really believed this was my life, he came into it for a reason and I had to figure everything out to make it work.

Stuck trying to make it work there was a time during a transition of me switching birth control that I had become pregnant again. Family and friends weren't happy for me. I was blinded by love and they knew there was no promising future for us. I stood away from them because of their judgmental comments. In their opinion, having another baby was a mistake. My ego didn't want to hear anything. One morning, I started spotting blood and went to the doctor. The doctor said, "I can't find the baby's heartbeat, you need an ultrasound." The ultrasound technician advised, "the baby stopped growing last week." I didn't understand what that meant and so I asked her, "Is the baby ok?" She replied, "there's no heartbeat." My first reaction was disbelief followed by a startling cry. I went back to my doctor with the report, she hugged me. She told me, "take some time off work and the miscarriage should happen in a few days...It will be a period from hell." She was right! I bled so much that I fainted. Sammy slapped my face hard to wake me up. I became conscious and crawled to my bed. He called my doctor and she instructed him to, "go get her a cheeseburger." It was morning time, he told me he had to insist to the fast food restaurant to make it. As I was lifeless at home, I prayed in hopes of getting better. Somehow, I managed to eat that cheeseburger. Energy came instantly, and I was able to clean up the horrific scene of blood from the miscarriage. My baby was gone now. The only thing I could do was to sit still and cry for hours. Seeing my husband sad made me cry even more. I put aside our differences and I was thankful that he was there for me during this time. He was the only one that showed me empathy and he never left my side. We loved each other, and the miscarriage brought us closer. I was left with a serious depression. I knew my life had to move on and my daughter needed me, the depression subsided within a few weeks. My faith in God grew a bit because I managed to get through everything.

One day, as Sammy was picking me up from work I was in shock when I saw him pulling up. My daughter was sitting on his lap in the driver seat. She had the biggest smile, but I yelled at him, "what are you doing?" He responded, "I'm teaching her how to drive." The danger he had put our three-year-old in, made me take him off the pick-up list from her daycare. The next day, he showed up at my job yelling at me in front of my co-workers. He asked, "why did you take me off the pick-up list?" I replied, "she needs to stay in school." He stormed out. When I picked up Camila later that day, the teachers looked scared. He had punched a hole in the door. I advised the owner to call the police. She didn't want to because he had threatened her. Going home was always hell. It was a place with no peace and plenty of war. I demanded for him to go to a detox center. He agreed to check in. On day four, he showed up at my job. His eyes were dilated, and he was pacing back and forth. He demanded the car keys and I gave it to him. Hours later, he picked me up and I was afraid of getting in the car. That day my friend asked me for a ride. I told her, "no" yet she insisted and said, "please, I need a ride." I raised my voice at this point and directly said, "it's not a good time!" She put her hand on the back-door handle and continued to insist making her way inside the car. As soon as we got in my husband floored it, his driving was erratic-making sharp turns, breaking hard and his body swaying side to side as the music was blaring. I had never experienced that before. We continued in route and picked up our daughter from daycare. I made sure her seat belt was fastened tightly. He took off again, everyone holding on for dear life. I prayed the whole time in the car for safety. We got to my friend's house as she jumped out she exclaimed, "never again!" I yelled back, "I told you!" I knew God was with us that day, and my prayers did work because we all got home safe.

Months went by and my marriage was at the brink of divorce. My husband's drug problem was out of control and he was always desperate for money. I feared him when he was itching for more drugs. I slept with my money and the car keys in my bra. I discovered that my daughter's birth certificate and social security card were hidden in a stuffed animal. Alarmed by this discovery I went in the drawer to search for mine, it wasn't there. He denied touching it, but I knew he was up to something. Everything he would say, I automatically assumed it was a lie. I had no trust in him. Having to defend myself and living this type of life with him was overwhelming. Threatening him and having full blown arguments was exhausting. My emotional state was anger and it had turned into a depression. My daughter would ignore our arguments or tell us to be quiet. She became immune to it. I asked myself, "do I try again to keep this family together?" I looked over to my daughter and was confused. I wanted her to grow up with her dad, he was her best friend. She had a bond with him. I would forgive him again but forgiving him only one last time was a promise I made to myself. He got clean again but not for long. I got smarter this time and went online to buy an at home drug test to prove him wrong. The package came a few days later and I hid it in the bathroom. It was a Friday evening, I told him, "I need your urine. I'm taking it to the drug test facility on Monday." He laughed. Without making it obvious, I went to the bathroom with his urine. My heart was racing. The test was like a pregnancy test, I had to wait a few minutes for the result. I knew the result, I just needed proof. The door started shaking and he was pounding. Yelling at me, "open the door!" I screamed out, "hold on, I'm using the bathroom!" As I opened the door, the test went flying out of my hand and hit him in the face. I was enraged with anger! I yelled, "there you go!" He said, "you're a dumb bitch, of course I would fail a drug test I smoked some marijuana." I yelled at him, "the test is for opiates! I'm done with you!" He packed up his belongings and before he could pick them up and leave I kicked the bags down the stairs. He said to me, "I left, you didn't kick me out." I shouted out in response, "okay, whatever makes you happy!" I did love him, but this relationship was officially over. I know, I know, about time. I divorced him and felt free at last!

Fast forward and now, I'm twenty-six-years-old. At this point I began dating again, and I got dropped off home by my new boyfriend. Putting the key into the door lock, I felt this fear come over me. As I was turning the doorknob, I was pushed from behind inside and as I turned around, Sammy slammed the door behind us asking me, "Who was that?" I said, "Nobody." He punched my eye and I threw myself over the couch. I wanted to be overly dramatic, so he could leave me alone. I was screaming, and he pushed me on the couch. He got on top of me and put his hands around my neck. I knew he was overpowering me, I closed my eyes and prayed. He stopped, released my neck and ran out of the house. I thanked God for saving my life. I knew the police could give me a protective order, but this guy was on a different level and a piece of paper wouldn't deter him. My mom and family were moving to Florida. I had to decide whether to stay or move with them. This sense of urgency kicked in, I knew I had to go far away. My ego gave me thoughts of fear. Fear of starting over, leaving family behind and not having enough money to move. But this sense of urgency to leave kicked out fear. I believe now that

God helped me with the decision to leave town. The safety of myself and my daughter became the number one priority. While packing and planning it became real, I was leaving. I was angry with my ex-husband for all the nonsense he had put me through. I allowed him to see our daughter one last time. Camila knew we were leaving town, but she kept the secret from him as instructed to do so. At the end of the visit, she hugged him and said, "bye." I was repeating the pattern of what I went through with my own father and my own goodbye. I thought saying goodbye one last time, would make her happy but the reality of it was her heart was broken. Weeks later, Sammy found out we left town. He saw a for rent sign on the window of our old apartment, he called me with concern. I had a vengeful attitude and thought that's what he deserved. I told him, "live your life with the pain of failing your family."

Starting my life over in a new state was a must. I worked and was saving up money for our own place. I felt guilty because my daughter lived in a dysfunctional household because of us. She was a strong little girl. Always did well in school, she had good behavior and seemed to be ok. At night, I would scratch her back and tell her, "I love you" as she fell asleep. I made sure she felt safe and had her needs met. I pushed my feelings of grief to the side. I had a heart to heart with myself, I was trying to convince myself to get out of this mindset of despair. I needed to appreciate the fact that we were safe. Telling myself, we're living the Florida lifestyle, just be happy! But happiness seemed out of reach, I felt lonely, sad and lost. When the sun was down, I felt a little happier. I was depressed. I prayed for a good man, I thought that was what I needed. Eventually, I met a new guy named Frank. God answered my prayer. He was young, cute, good hearted and very funny. We dated for over a year, fell in love and moved in together. Camila didn't like

Frank being in our life. She would give Frank an attitude. She already knew that her dad and I were never going to be together because we couldn't get along. She had a rough time accepting that. I decided to buy her a puppy. She was lonely, and the dog became her everything. I gave Frank attitude as well. Since I was older than him, I expected a lot from him. He was falling short on doing things the right way, at least that's how I felt. We would argue over dumb things and my anger would come out. On the weekends, we had family and friends come over, it was party time! We would drink alcohol, smoke marijuana-laughing was my stress reliever. My house was party central, no worries, no fear just a group of like minded folks.

I asked myself, "my thirties are coming, am I ready to unravel my mess?" I recapped my twenties in my mind, there were good times and plenty of bad times. All I could do was focus on the negative experiences because it had emotional pain attached to it. My negative experiences didn't define who I was, but it was my truth that I lived. My divorce was like a death, I was never going to be with him again. I loved him, and I knew our time was up. My miscarriage was a real death I had endured. In my heart, I always felt like he was going to be a boy. The miscarriage was the most traumatic experience in my adulthood. Having a lot of emotions not dealt with, created festering anger. I was angry at my ex-husband, and myself. Being angry at him for not putting in any effort to make the relationship work. I was mad at myself for wasting time trying to change him. He wasn't the man that I needed, I married him without knowing him. Listening to my ego, lead me to unnecessary pain. The "I can do it" thinking caused me to sacrifice my own happiness. My ego was in control for far too long. All the poor decisions I had made were based on fear. Fear of being wrong and thinking I would never find someone to love me again. My marriage had left me feeling frustrated, lost and all I could do was judge myself. I chose not to take care of myself and that's when I stopped loving myself. I needed to talk to someone about my feelings, but I pretended to be happy in front of others. I chose to suffer on the inside because I didn't know any better. I lived two lives. Smoking marijuana calmed the ticking of the time bomb inside of me. I had to stay focused on my daughter Camila, she gave me the strength to keep going. I kept busy with her by taking her to the park, library and eating out. If I had known then that prayer and depending on God could've saved me from all the anguish, dropping to my knees would've been done all the time. Unfortunately, I only prayed when I was in fear. At this point in my life, I wasn't ready to unravel anything. I thought I would just get over it.

CHAPTER 3

THE TURN-A-BOUT

Faith in God is having complete trust with an unshakeable confidence for who he is. Faith has nothing to do with seeing. It's about the inner knowing that comes from your spirit. Your spirit's function is spiritual and was given to you to contact and receive God. Fully surrendering to God is never forced upon you. Eventually, your soul will be ready for healing and you'll want to surrender to God. Surrendering means to give up control of your life and acknowledging that God is in control. He wants you to surrender your mind, body and soul. As humans, we allow our mind and our will to dictate how we live. When we're in control, we exhaust ourselves. The good news is, when you're ready to surrender God is always ready for you. He wants you to start living again. Do you believe that God is real? If yes, Amen. If you're not sure, you can pray and ask for a sign. When your confirmation comes, accept the truth. I'm a visual person and when I pray to Jesus, I visualize us together - we're at a beach, on a mountain, or even at a campsite. I feel more of a connection if I see him. There are no rules on how to pray. Whatever works for you, go for it. The power of prayer is real. He's listening and ready to help you. God loves you. *"And he saith unto them, Because of your little faith: for verily I say unto you, If ye have faith as a grain of mustard seed, ye shall say unto this mountain, Remove hence to yonder place; and it shall remove; and nothing shall be impossible unto you." Matthew 17:20 (American Standard Version)*

Trusting and believing in God is life changing. It's up to your will to decide if you're ready to surrender or not? The mind, body and soul can take only up to so much pain. I'm here to point the way to God, Jesus and the Holy Spirit for healing. I truly want you to heal from your past and present traumas. I believe miracles can happen in your life when you say, "Father, I'm ready for a total surrender... I surrender my mind, body and soul to you. I will accept Jesus as my Lord and Savior." These words must come from your heart, you must mean it. Only then, the Holy Spirit will connect to your spirit. God wants everything from you! *"Neither present your members unto sin as instruments of unrighteousness; but present yourselves unto God, as alive from the dead, and your members as instruments of righteousness unto God." Romans 6:13 (American Standard Version)* God's will is to save you, heal you and give you a new life. You will feel alive again because of God's power. You have a choice to make, you can take the long path or the short path to victory. The short path is surrendering everything all at once followed by a baptism. I was on the long path because fear led my life.

I will explain in detail what God wants from you. A mind is a part of the soul. The mind has two parts: an intellectual side and an emotional side. Surrendering the intellectual side of your mind means to change the "what" you think and the "how" you think. Surrendering your emotional side of your mind means to give your pain, fear and ego to God. A renewal of the mind helps you keep your mind focused on Jesus. A body is the physical part of a human. To surrender your body means you become God's temple, the Holy Spirit will dwell in you. His purpose is to convict your sins and guide you into all truth. If you hold on to unforgiveness and any other sins in your heart, the Holy Spirit will grieve and retreat from helping you. You must confess and repent of your sins. Then Jesus will forgive you and the Holy Spirit will be able to do his work in you. A soul is the non-physical part of a human. The surrendering of your soul is a vow made to the Lord, that a decision has been made to bind your soul with his by accepting him as your Lord and Savior. God loves you, he sent Jesus to save you from your own punishment that you deserved for sinning and to secure wholeness and healing. His resurrection was to confirm salvation and his identity as the Son of God. God wants you to fully surrender to make you whole. You will be saved, forgiven, renewed, given a new life, given an eternal life, and healed physically and spiritually. After surrendering, getting baptized is important. A baptism is a testimony to God and to the world that you will live as an overcomer in your new life.

Accepting Jesus will bring a healing process to you or an instant healing. An instant healing is God speeding up the process, which is called a miracle. As you get to know Jesus, your healing and peace will grow. To create a wonderful relationship with Jesus, you must focus on talking, listening, praying and reading the word. He hears you and when you listen to him by doing the right things, your life will be blessed more and more. Jesus is worthy of your worship, worthy of your time, and remember he died for you. God has given himself to you in many ways. The Holy Spirit helps you by being your counselor, advocator and encourager. Jesus helps you by giving you his love, peace, hope, salvation and joy. In addition, God has given us guardian angel(s) to help us and comfort us. You have a choice to accept all of this as truth or not. Believing in a higher power can make the ultimate difference in your life. To Rule Your Life means, you must act on a decision to change something about yourself or about a situation, for a more meaningful life. Change is good. Whenever you're ready to fully surrender to God, the beginning of chapter six has a meditation and surrender prayer for you. You can always come back to this chapter later.

"Being therefore justified by faith, we have peace with God through our Lord Jesus Christ."
Romans 5:1 (American Standard Version)

On my thirtieth birthday, I wasn't excited about this new decade. I just didn't know how to be happy. A lot of thinking came after my birthday. I knew I had to start somewhere, to get to the place of true happiness. Letting go of bad childhood memories was easier said than done. My twenties were a roller coaster ride which had left me with additional weight on my shoulders. I was still angry and only a few people saw that side of me. The anger would come out when I had to defend myself. One day, I checked the mail and I received a collection bill. The information on it was confusing, it was a medical bill from a facility in Arkansas. Confusing because I never had surgery done in Arkansas. I called the billing department, she confirmed that the information was with my identity. A flashback came to my mind and I remembered that my original birth certificate and social security card were once missing. I had ordered new copies a while back, but the originals were never found. Did my ex-husband sell my identity? I called him, and he denied selling it. But he did confess that he had possession of it and lost it. I screamed at him, "how can you do this to me?" He said, "if it makes you feel better, I lost mine too." Fury came over me, I was feeling flames coming out of my ears because I knew the truth. I hung up on him. Instant worry came and with that worry my body reacted physically with lots of diarrhea. My life was turned upside down.

Survivor mode kicked in and I had to focus on what was currently going on. I refused to allow someone to use my identity and live my life. Ideas came to my mind and I had to collect all evidence against this thief. Clearing my name was going to take time, patience, and resources. I asked my boss, "can I fix this mess during work hours?" Thankfully she said "yes." I used my jobs resources like phone, fax and computer for six months. First, I made a police report in the same city where the hospital was. Next, I called all local utility companies, I found out I had active accounts. Now I knew the address where the thief lived. Calling the DMV fraud department was my next move. I had them fax over "my" state ID. With some more digging, I found out I had a warrant out for "my" arrest. This "I" had a DUI and child endangerment charge. To top it off "I" also had a car under my name that was in the impound. Running my credit report was another idea, which led to discovering more of a mess. Many credit cards with delinquent high balances. I called the IRS to run my social security number, they said I was working in two states. I owed the IRS back taxes too. Now, I'm responsible to fix this disaster. Mentally and emotionally I was shutting down. I had always felt like I could do things on my own but this time I couldn't. All the stress caused my chest to hurt. I decided to pray to God for help, I needed his strength to continue.

I lost a good amount of weight because I was worried that my freedom was at risk. I had many phone calls to make to guarantee my freedom. I started with the courthouse to get the warrant lifted. In the process of fixing everything, there were times I got disconnected, transferred and given the runaround. I felt as if I was running a marathon and jumping through hurdles the whole way. With God's help, I was successful in collecting forty-seven pages of pure evidence. Now I just needed someone to arrest her. The Local authorities from my town and the town in Arkansas couldn't assist me. I was told, they had more important things to do. Now, I'm talking to myself. "What now? Do I go and do a citizen's arrest? No wait, I will call the FBI!" I found the local office near the town in Arkansas, I asked for their fax number. I called back to speak to an available agent, Mr. Smith was an angel sent from God. I said, "hello sir, as we speak, I'm sending forty-seven pages of evidence through the fax." "A woman in your town, has stolen my identity and I need you to arrest her." He said, "I'm sitting near the fax, this is a lot of information. I will look this over and call you tomorrow." The next day, he called me and said, "I have her in custody." I screamed out, "Oh my God!" I was shaking and had tears of joy. Thanking him over and over, as I was jumping up and down. I felt some weight come off my shoulders and peace come over me. I thanked God for everything. Eventually, every fraud account or concern was reversed, canceled, voided, or released. My goal was accomplished, and my identity was better than ever. The result for the thief who lived my life, was deported back to Mexico. She was in the U.S. illegally and had two small children. I was sad about her two kids, I didn't know what was going to happen to them. However, I had to press charges. She committed many crimes and had to be stopped.

Through the fighting of my identity theft I finally received some great news, I was pregnant! Frank, Camila and I were excited, we were welcoming a boy! Our son Isaac was born in the summertime. I'm fortunate to be an at home mom. Frank was the breadwinner as I focused on raising the kids, keeping the house in order and whomever needed help I was there for them. But dragging my emotional baggage was heavy and I was clueless on how to obtain peace. Smoking marijuana on the weekends led to a daily habit for Frank and I. Smoking helped me forget about my issues, I hid them well. I didn't know how to put my needs first, that's what happens when you don't love yourself. I started to feel my conscience bothering me. I didn't know that God was nudging me, I just ignored the thoughts. As time went on it was time for my daughter to start middle school. In those years she had distanced herself from the family. I assumed she's just growing up, that's what preteens do. As a parent, I lacked communication and I needed to spend more quality time with her. I didn't know how to bond with her at that age. She didn't want hugs from me anymore and she could care less about going to the park or library. Her stepdad would try to reach out to her, but she wasn't having it. She tested me with bad behavior, but I wasn't having it. I spoke to her and asked, "what's wrong?" She replied, "nothing." I told her, "I can't help you, if you don't talk to me." Report card time came around and I suggested to give her money for all her good grades. I remember that idea really made her smile. I decided to teach her how to do her own laundry and showed her how to cook and bake certain things; this way of bonding came natural to me. She liked the idea of becoming independent, and I knew that. Camila has a strong will, she knows what she wants and goes for it, she always has. Although I bonded in this way with her, I still chose to begin to read books on mindfulness and happiness. My goal was to be more present and involved with my children.

My boyfriend and I tried to be good role models, but we did argue a lot. Compared to my first marriage, these problems were nothing. I wanted his attention and demanded respect. Frank would womanize when we were out in public. He would deny checking out other women, but he did it right in my face. I made it very clear to him, that I demand respect! As we would argue, my anger would come out by yelling loud. I had bad habits from my past and thought that was the only way to get my point across. He was stubborn and wouldn't admit his wrong doing. After we both did some overreacting, he would admit his wrongs and apologize. Sometimes, I would apologize for my big mouth and other times I wouldn't. I felt like I was defending myself so why apologize. Us making up was always good, we would bond in the garage smoking, the usual. When I was sober, I was busy helping others. I would do favors or give the best advice to my family and friends. There was this inner wisdom that I shared, sometimes I would surprise myself, my focus was to make sure they're doing good. Their happiness brought me satisfaction plus it was a distraction from my own problems. I was invested emotionally with their problems because I did care. They depended on my problem solving a bit too much though, to the point that I began to feel overwhelmed. Little by little I pushed some family and friends away. I even pushed friends away that weren't dependent on me. I became self-aware and I knew I had to stop judging myself and stop allowing fear to run my life. Fear of change is real. I made a bold decision that it was time to Rule My Life. At this moment, my spiritual journey was summoned, and I had no idea that my willingness for change had put me on the right path. I no longer wanted to live with anger, shame or pain. I wasn't sure what route to take to get rid of the unresolved emotions brewing in me. I felt like screaming! What's wrong with me I would think, why did I feel so unhappy.

One day, my son Isaac was sick. He had a fever and I took him to the doctor. The doctor said he had a throat infection and prescribed penicillin and fever reducer. Two days passed, his fever was not under control, ranging from one-hundred-and-one to one-hundred-and-four. I noticed my son's lips were starting to chap and he was weak. My family and I took him back to his doctor. The doctor said, "his throat looks bad and now his ears are infected too. He needs the children's hospital." My heart dropped. We drove to the emergency room. My son was put on IV immediately. The main doctor couldn't diagnose him, he had to call in a specialist. My son's symptoms were a throat, ear, and urine infection. With that came a rash that started to develop throughout his body. His lips were worsening, and his fever was still high. I was crying and pacing back and forth, wanting answers. My poor baby was helpless. I decided to pray to God, asking him to help my son. I had some faith in prayer because when I prayed in the past everything did work out. Hours later, I had three doctors come to me and circle around me. The specialist said, "I suspect either Mono or The Kawasaki Disease. I have to run further test to get a final diagnosis." I asked, "doctor, I hope medicine is a solution?" She replied, "Mono is treatable with antibiotics, and the Kawasaki Disease requires plasma." I was grateful to hear that there was a remedy, but my son was looking worse; the rash now covered his body and his lips started to bleed from being chapped. He was crying, I was crying. He had various wires and machines attached to him. He was weak and all I could do was hold his hand. The nurse came in to get another urine sample. My poor baby boy screamed so loud because of the pain. Helpless I tried to comfort him by telling him, "you will be alright, momma loves you."

What seemed like an eternity the specialist finally came back to update me. She said, "he has the Kawasaki Disease. It's a rare disease that can affect his heart. As we speak his immune system is failing." She continued, "we are defrosting the plasma, but it takes 24 hours. We will do everything we can to help him." Now, we had to wait 24 hours in hopes that the plasma was the answer. Praying again for healing and begging God to save him. He was my only son and I adored him. My family and I were in despair. The next morning, Frank and I received a phone call from my aunt. She said, "God wants me to come to the hospital to pray over your son." And of course, my answer was, "yes, please." When she arrived, she declared, "Jesus is going to heal him!" She pointed out a trash can in the room and continued "The trash can must go. The devil is hiding in there." I was afraid to pick up the trash can, so I kicked it with my foot as I opened the door and left it in the hallway. I didn't know what to believe but, I knew I wanted my son healed. We maneuvered all the wires and machines because God wanted me to hold my three-year-old boy. My aunt began to pray, and she started speaking in tongues. That's when a human speaks a language that's unknown to speaker and listener. It was the holy spirit speaking and his power went through all of us. I felt a peace come over me, and joy filled my heart. As my aunt was praying, she touched my sons head. I'm looking at my son's body, his rash started to disappear right before my eyes. Spot by spot. My faith increased, I knew a healing was happening. We were all blessed. I shouted, "thank you, thank u Jesus!" She ended the prayer with, "he is healed in Jesus name, Amen!" Everyone said, "Amen!" I put my son back in the bed, I called for the nurse. I asked her to check his temperature. From one-hundred-three point eight, it had dropped to one-hundred point eight. I began feeling grateful and had an inner knowing that everything was alright. My son was now recovering!

But Jesus wasn't done. My aunt told me, "I have a message from Jesus. Jesus wants you to read Psalm 23." I said, "okay." I thanked her for everything, and she left. My son called for me and said, "mom, I'm hungry." I got him breakfast and fed him pancakes and sausage. He ate most of it. The specialist walked in and noticed his improvements. The fever and rash were gone. She checked his ears and throat, he had no infection. He was just a little weak. The doctor had a puzzled look and she said, "the plasma is still defrosting. I don't think he needs it." I told her, "I don't think he needs it either. My son got healed from a prayer, Jesus healed him." She didn't say anything about that. Instead she said, "tomorrow morning I will release him, if everything checks out." I said, "ok." At this moment, it was just my son and I in the hospital room. As he was sleeping, I decided to research my message from Jesus. The first sentence was, **"Jehovah is my shepherd; I shall not want." Psalm 23:1 (American Standard Version)** I believe that God used my son as a wakeup call for me. Unfortunately, I had to see it before I believed that God's healing power was real. I was ready to Rule My Life and give God my yucky feelings. The Holy Spirit was present again, I could feel his presence. Getting on my knees was a must and I said, "Father, I surrender my mind and body to you. I thank you for saving my son's life. I thank you for everything. I will focus on you and I invite your Holy Spirit to stay with me, Amen." I began to weep. God's plan for me was to discover, recognize and receive his healing power. A warm sensation went through my body and peace came over me. I felt good and I was optimistic about my future. The next morning, the doctor released my son. I took him to a heart specialist for testing, it was required because he did have the Kawasaki Disease. His heart wasn't affected, he was one-hundred percent healthy.

Life was going well. My kids were always first on my list. I was used to putting myself last for everything, my mindset needed help. I desperately needed my journey to start, spiritual growth was a must. I envisioned myself climbing my mountain because I wanted to reach the top and feel complete. I made the decision to stop hiding behind marijuana. I was enthusiastic about learning about myself and learning about many subjects, I decided to go to the library. Always praying for the Holy Spirit to guide me, he would lead me to the perfect book that I needed. Reading different subjects in search of a quick solution to get my "aha moment". I would start with the last page hoping my answer was there. In those moments I learned about the Holy Spirit, faith, peace, Jesus, angels, mindful thinking, and positive thinking. Most of the things I read, took me some time to process because it was a lot of information. I applied some things that I had learned but I knew something was still wrong with me, I didn't feel peace daily. At times feeling restless, sad and I wasn't sure what direction to go in. I felt incomplete. I prayed to God for a sign for my next step. The very next day, we got invited to attend a Christian church service. We were there on time. The pastor called my whole family up to the front. He began to read a verse from the bible. *"Our fathers sinned, and are not; And we have borne their iniquities." Lamentations 5:7 (American Standard Version)* He exclaimed, "we must pray for your generational curse to be removed, it's removed through salvation!" The curse we had, was brought upon us for using and believing in witchcraft. God will punish you and generations after you, if you idolize anything. Salvation is confessing and believing that Jesus is your Lord and Savior. Salvation also refers to, a deliverance from evil, a life of freedom, and it will protect you from earthly dangers. The pastor prayed for all of us. I was ready and willing to accept Jesus Christ as my Lord and Savior. We were saved! I surrendered my soul to the Lord. I had surrendered my mind and body already. So now that made it a total surrender for me. Jesus Christ was the change of direction that I needed to follow. The best way to describe how I felt was, having no worries. I had received healing for my soul. It felt like a veil was removed from my face. My conscious was awoken and I knew it was the Holy Spirit in me.

Surrendering EVERYTHING to God all at once can save you time. I wish I had listened to my heart's desires. Instead, I allowed fear to be in charge and I surrendered a part at a time. God did bless my life, I was less angry and felt happier. Now it was all about Jesus. Living for the Lord gave me purpose. Praying for a renewed mind was needed daily. Plus depending on the Holy Spirit was a must. Sometimes, my mind would wander off when I was trying to stay living in the moment. My attitude towards some situations or problems were calmer instead of frantic. Within time, I learned to respond to things versus react to things. I chose to apply what I learned because I wanted our quality of life to be better. Nevertheless, I felt God nudging me again. I was avoiding a pressing feeling in my conscience. I knew exactly what that was all about, but I decided to ignore it. I focused on the peace that I received when I asked the Holy Spirit to guide me. But the peace wouldn't stay long. On one special day, I was shocked to find out I was having another baby. I knew she would be my last, I was in my late thirties. No complications during pregnancy or birth. I had another girl, we named her Sophia! Now, I was a mother of three. Frank and I decided to get married, it was time to stop living in sin. Doing the right thing always made me feel good. Little by little, I was willing to change different things in my life. Breaking patterns was on my agenda. I had a "lack mentality" - holding on to old belongings and not knowing how to shop for myself. I knew in time my old thinking would be changed. Also, having more quality time with my kids was a must. On Wednesdays, it was breakfast for dinner at home. The kids loved that idea. After we ate, we would spend quality time together by playing board games, doing a puzzle or taking a walk. On the weekends, we did a lot of fun things together. Our summer vacations were the best, we stayed at new hotels on the beach. Appreciating the moments of bonding with them. God had blessed me with three healthy and beautiful kids. My husband and I would bond too, we loved each other dearly.

The bliss continued and one day, I received a call from my dad, him and my grandfather wanted to visit. They came on the same weekend of Sophia's first birthday. It was one of the best weekends I ever had. Our father/daughter relationship had just begun, I was thrilled. We talked, laughed, ate and the time went by slow. The little girl in me felt safe, I had my dad and my grandpa. I didn't want this great feeling to go away. Unfortunately, they had to leave. My dad and I had an over the phone relationship. He's a funny guy, always saying jokes. He wanted to hear about my day and hear stories about his grandkids. I asked him questions about his past. As he would share stories and he would get emotional. A few months had passed, and my dad called me with bad news. He had throat cancer. He was scared and had to go through many challenges to stay alive. I would call him to keep his hopes up with plenty of encouragement. After the phone call, I would feel drained emotionally. I felt sorry for him, and sorry for myself. He couldn't catch a break from life and had to deal with a major hurdle. Our relationship had finally started to take off, now he was facing a possibility of losing his life. I still needed him. His other kids needed him too. This was not fair! He was trying to make his wrongs right, with so much to live for but he couldn't think beyond his sickness. He had many tests to take and eventually surgery would happen. Crying was my temporary release and prayer was my permanent solution. He became dependent on me to get through his day. I was committed to help him see this through for I love him dearly.

My fortieth birthday was around the corner and I sat to recap my thirties. A mother of three, I was married, I was saved, I had a big house, cars, pets, money in the bank, good health and felt satisfied on my self-help progress. I really did think my journey was almost over but come to find out I was nowhere near the top of my mountain. I still felt heaviness in my heart, I had no peace or joy. The reason that peace didn't stay with me was because I had unforgiveness in my heart. Holding on to it was by choice, it was attached to my baggage that was filled with emotional pain. I continued to pray for answers, I needed peace in my life. The Holy Spirit had nudged me because he wanted me to let go of the negative emotions and to forgive those who had hurt me. I was working backwards. I didn't fully surrender my mind and body to God. Apparently, I had given him the intellect part of my mind and not the emotional part. The feeling of an emotion comes from the mind, heart and body acting as one. My emotions were everywhere, and I was affecting my mind and body. To move forward, I knew I had to speak my truth, I must confess and repent of my sins, forgive those who hurt me and then surrender my mind and body. Jesus will then forgive me, and the Holy Spirit will continue doing his work in me. "How do I speak my truth?" Emotions were stirred up of shame, abandonment, and hurt. It was hard to swallow, I had a knot feeling in my throat. I had a lot of resentment that turned into frustration. The frustration overwhelmed me, and I had to scream loud. I screamed so loud that a roar came out of me. I scared myself because I sounded like a real lion, a lioness. The scream alleviated the pressure I was feeling but I knew it was time to speak up and let go. I prayed to God to renew my mind again and to help me forgive others. I needed some courage to jump over my last hurdle, which took me into my new decade.

CHAPTER 4

WILLING TO FORGIVE

Being a child of God should be a beautiful experience but for some it's not so beautiful. You're here on earth to learn from all your experiences. Some of you may have been raised by your parent(s), guardian(s), the system or raised yourself. Each circumstance has given you a one-of-a-kind experience. Your childhood experiences may have been rough and/or hell because of someone's wrongdoing. Adulthood may bring rough experience's too, causing you to feel some type of way and create resentment. Your soul is always ready to forgive, but your ego will hold you back if you allow it to. To hold on to unforgiveness means you must carry the burden(s) with you throughout your lifetime. Unforgiveness can affect your health and steal your peace, leaving you with no joy. Forgiving others doesn't give that person a pass, God will handle them accordingly. To forgive is when you can stop feeling angry and/or resentful toward someone for a mistake and/or any hurt against you. Forgiveness is a word that some people don't want to think about. Some may have claimed that they have forgiven others but still hold a grudge. That's not true forgiveness. Speaking your truth and going through the hurt, clears the way for forgiveness. Being willing to forgive and giving it to God is the way to let go, God will figure out the rest. Some may have truly forgiven those who have hurt them and Amen to that. Forgiving others is about you, so you can live a life with no hate in your heart and stop sinning. If you're ready to forgive yourself or someone, you need to confess and repent to the Lord. He will then forgive you too.

"For if ye forgive men their trespasses, your heavenly Father will also forgive you. But if ye forgive not men their trespasses, neither will

your Father forgive your trespasses." Matthew 6:14-15 (American Standard Version)

I am here to help you forgive others or to forgive yourself. It's my timing when to release the forgiveness. I can choose an instant release and you're set free. Sometimes, I don't do it instantly and that's because I see your heart. You may still have resentment or anger. Holding on to unforgiveness is not a willing to forgive state of mind. Forgiving is releasing them to me and letting go of its hold on you. Peace and Joy in your heart is the indicator of a forgiving heart. You can start new with me, you will be given full forgiveness.

Happy fortieth birthday to me. I had come a long way, but I knew there was more spiritual growing needed. I prayed to Jesus, I had visualized us at a campsite. There was a big campfire and Jesus was sitting on his throne. As he sat and listened, I told him I was ready to speak about my past and I wanted to let go of fear. I wrapped up my fear in a red cloth and I gave it to Jesus. He took it from me and threw it into the campfire. The next morning, I woke up without fear and I had given myself permission to go through my toughest experience. My visual prayer worked for me. It was hard to accept that I was a victim of molestation because I was in denial my whole life. Molestation is to subject a child to sexual contact, exposure of genitalia and/or pornographic material. My experience was sexual contact and exposure of genitalia and I had to admit that to myself. Acknowledging it became my truth. Questioning, "why would the men in my life do that to me?" At that moment, I felt like telling them off! They had disrespected me and made me feel shameful. Now I felt it was a must to tell my mom what had happened many years ago. This was one of the hardest things I had to do. She came by my house and I sat her down. For years I avoided this moment, I never wanted to give her my burdens. I began to speak my truth. I told her my childhood molestation stories and awkward moments. My mom asked, "why didn't you tell me?" I replied, "I don't know...I didn't know how to talk about it." We prayed and hugged. The heaviness I felt was lighter, but I knew I wasn't done.

My dad and I were over the phone buddies. His throat surgery was scheduled, and he was afraid that he wouldn't be able to talk anymore. He completed everything the doctor suggested which included the surgery, radiation and chemotherapy. Yes, he had completed all the cancer treatments needed as advised by medical professionals, but he gave God the credit for getting cancer out of his life. After his surgeries he was left with many complications and still needed more healing. He couldn't swallow food, drink liquids or talk how he used to. In the process of trying to heal, he lost a lot of weight. He was about eighty-eight pounds. Throughout his recovery, he was still doing heroin, smoking marijuana and cigarettes. I guess, he didn't learn his lesson. Keeping him positive was hard because all he could see was his problems. God would use me to pass messages to him, to give him messages of hope. One day, I was talking to him and he said, "I want to tell you something." I was listening. He said, "I want you to forgive me, for not ever being there for you." He was crying and so was I. I replied to him, "I forgive you." And he followed with, "I love you." Naturally I said, "I love you too." I'm glad he was able to clear up some of his guilt that he was holding in. My conscience started to bother me, and I knew I had to let go of the guilt that I was feeling. I wanted to ask certain family members to forgive me too. I started with my dad. I said, "can you forgive me for not visiting you?" He said, "you are there for me just in a different way, but I forgive you." I was overdue on visiting him and feared seeing him skinny and sick. I always avoided seeing any family members in the hospital and especially a bedridden dad. That was something I had to work on. I told myself, "It's not about me, it's about him." When I was finally by my dad's side, I ran my fingers through his hair as I was praying for him. I felt sorrow in my heart, his life had come to this. He was stuck and couldn't see a way out. He needed another healing from God. I was grateful that I was able to be there for him, he was happy.

I was led by the Holy Spirit to correct relationships in my life, starting with my marriage. For a while, I had been working on myself but my relationship with my husband needed to get right. I started with prayer and asked Jesus for help. I had to take responsibility for my wrong doings. Feeling incomplete during our relationship, had showed up in my attitude. Having a nasty attitude towards the man I loved, had to stop immediately. I was older than him and I expected a whole lot from him. I wanted things done my way and to my liking. My biggest want was respect, I had no room for tolerating disrespect. Experiencing disrespect in my past put me on defense mode and gave me the excuse to lash out. We were in a cycle of disrespecting each other. I was trying to break patterns of my bad behavior that I had created in myself. I already knew that I couldn't change my husband. My focus was to respond calmly all the time. I was tested many times and had learned to think before I speak. My husband learned how to respect me because God had nudged him to change. When God nudges you, you should listen to your conscience. The Holy Spirit convicts us. If we continuously ignore him, the Holy Spirit's fire will quench, and he won't be available. That is one sin that God doesn't forgive. I am thankful that prayer helped my husband and I. Focusing on the today brought a new perspective for me and I learned to appreciate him more. I told my husband, "you met me damaged, insecure and you had to deal with my nasty attitude. I am sorry, I am asking you to forgive me." He did. He asked for forgiveness as well and like he I also forgave him, we hugged and embraced one another.

I started going around to some family and friends asking them to forgive me for any harm I may have caused. Especially to my oldest daughter. She went through the emotional roller coaster ride with me; from living in a dysfunctional home as a small child to living with a broken mom as years had passed- although of course that wasn't my intention. I explained to her, "I couldn't give you what I didn't have. I didn't love myself enough and it affected how I showed love. I did the best that I knew how. Can you please forgive me?" Camila replied, "I forgive you. The thing I'm sad about is, you won't let me have another dog." I exclaimed, "what! I'm pouring out my heart to you." I asked her, "do you have any hard feelings?" She replied, "I know you tried your best and you never forgot about me, like my dad." Camilla and I had the same "daddy isn't here" story. The cycle had continued to her generation and had to be broken. Her dad never acknowledged her after we moved to Florida. I told her, "forgive your dad, and please don't follow the path I went through. Save yourself time and misery." She wasn't ready to forgive him. I pray every day that she will be willing to forgive him and let go of any pain. We gave each other a big hug. By the way, she got a big "no" about her dog request. I was being hard on myself for not being a perfect mom. I know now, I did better than I thought. Letting go of the guilt felt good. A parent's duty is to communicate, protect, love, support, teach and create as many great memories as possible. Time goes by quickly and it's never too late to start doing whatever it is that you may have been slacking in. I try not to smother my kids these days. I can proudly say, I'm a pretty good mother.

It was time to look myself in the mirror. Forgiveness was long overdue. I had carried with me plenty of guilt, and disappointments. I wanted to learn how to put myself first in a non-selfish way. Abandoning myself physically, emotionally and mentally had to stop. I was done punishing myself with the "I'm not good enough" and the "there's not enough" mentality. There was no time for self-pity and the new me must show up. I started with speaking out loud and acknowledging that I had caused some of my own pain. Similarly, I acknowledged to myself that as a child, it was not my fault for any bad experiences. I became aware and saw myself through a new set of eyes. I noted my skin was dry, my hair was damaged, and I was thirty pounds overweight. To me that was an abandonment, abandonment of thy self. I prayed to Jesus to help me process everything, to help me get my authentic self-back. Correspondingly, I was willing to forgive myself. The time had come to love myself again. I asked my mirror image to, "please forgive me." I cried like a baby. I released the unforgiveness that I had toward myself. Willing to let go became an empowering moment for me. Fear left, and love filled my heart. I thanked Jesus for everything. Moments after, thoughts came to me and I started to understand myself. I didn't feel worthy throughout my life because my dad didn't instill in me any self-worth. He neglected to show me love causing me to mirror that neglect and it made me feel not worthy of love. Still I take responsibility for making bad decisions in my life. Making your child feel loved and important will build strong character. They'll be confident in who they are and won't have to go out searching to fulfill any needs because they'll have it already. I started to feel lively which brought motivation and I knew everything was coming together. A major makeover was in the works, I was feeling amazing. I had a new attitude with an optimistic mindset but still needed help with my mind staying on track.

My mind needed help with my thoughts of resentment. I had resentment towards some male family members. I had many questions come to mind, "why should I have to forgive these pervert men? Should I confront them now or let them get away with it?" "Why should I forgive anyone who has hurt me?" "Do I want to drag this emotional baggage around forever?" "Is it about me or them?" As I questioned this in my mind a knowing came to me, that God loves me. He will deal with everyone who had hurt me. In my forgiveness prayer, I visualized each person as I said their name and I gave them to Jesus. I asked Jesus to forgive me too. In my surrender prayer, I gave him my mind and body. I fully surrendered everything to God and God's promise was to give me a new life. At that moment, I felt as if shackles were released from my feet. My locked-up emotions disappeared when I forgave, and Jesus forgave me too. I felt Jesus healing power healing my broken heart and my victim state of mind. I felt alive! The Holy Spirit filled me up with peace and joy in my heart. I haven't felt this way since I was a little girl. I'm back! Weeping and weeping, I was crying for my younger self, and crying for my present self. I was left with a sense of accomplishment, I did it! Forgiving others gave me the opportunity to focus on the present. I knew forgiveness occurred because when I would think about certain people, my reaction had changed from anger and resentment to feeling sorry for them, empathy. I began to include them in my prayers too. Since I was living in harmony with the Holy Spirit, I was given the fruit of the Holy Spirit; love, joy, peace, patience, kindness, goodness, faithfulness, gentleness, and self-control.

With this harmony came a great opportunity to get baptized. The baptism took place in my mom's swimming pool. As we stood there it was now my turn. The pastor said a prayer and the back of my head went in the water. I wanted to be a testimony to God and to the world that I will live as an overcomer in my new life. After the ceremony was over, we had a prayer inside. The pastor put his hand on my neck and said, "Jesus has already healed you, this is your confirmation." I was thankful to Jesus he healed me from my past and present traumas. Now, I was able to start living again. I was thrilled and happy to be truly blessed. The goal for me was to have only goodness flowing through my body, always having the Holy Spirit with me. I prayed every day for a renewed mind. Thoughts would come to me, that I had to work on retraining my mind. I decided to read more books on mindfulness and manifestation. I recommend watching the film, "The Secret" (2006). This showed me the power of manifesting. I manifested some things and boy did that spark some interest in me. I went around to family and friends giving them information to get their own manifestations started. I wanted to help them. If I can do it, they can do it. I was nowhere near mastering my mind, but I felt good about my progress. I heard family rumors going around that I was crazy and too positive. I was crazy because I had high hopes for everything. I believe that God gives us the authority to create our life, but he is the finisher in deciding what we get.

As time went by, I received sad news from my brother back home. My dad had passed away. He was living at home under hospice care and some family found him unresponsive. He had many complications, especially with his lungs. His throat was never fully healed either. He disregarded what doctors told him about no food allowed. He had a tube inserted and special milk for nutrients but chose solids-food. Most of the food would go straight to his lungs causing him to need an oxygen tank to help him breath. Having oxygen tanks in the home was dangerous. The danger came from my dad choosing to smoke cigarettes and marijuana while having the tanks in the same room. The family in that home lived in fear. Fear of the house blowing up and causing death to everyone. He didn't want to stop. The morning of his death, we believe he had heart failure. Seeing him at the wake was surreal. I was one of the first people to get there and tears came down my face as my memories of him flashed in my mind. I told him, "I love you forever." He was only fifty-seven and he didn't get to live out his purpose. He believed he was supposed to be a walking testimony. To tell other sick people he was a cancer survivor and that they can do it to. Months prior he had told me, "I'm living with plenty of regret. The regret that haunts me is the divorce with your mom." I replied, "let it go and forgive yourself." Of course, his other regrets were the drug use and him not being fully present in everyone's life. He left behind six children and nine grandchildren, all of us having a different relationship with him. We all grieved in our own way. I believe he made it to heaven, he had a good heart, just made poor decisions.

God's perfect timing for blessings come into your reality when you need it the most. For any unjust things that came into my life, God did give me ten folds. The ups and downs that I experienced had left me with a broken heart and a victim state of mind. I wish I had listened to my conscience when God spoke. I could've surrendered everything all at once to God and saved myself some time. He wanted my mind, body and soul and I eventually surrendered it all. Jesus healed my past and present traumas and I was able to start living again. I became one with him because my soul was yearning for him. I felt alive as if I was floating, with no heaviness wearing me down. I've learned a lot about myself and I'm thankful for my renewed mind. Every day I'm transforming, becoming a better person, I chose to live my life for God. I love myself and I'm emotionally healthy. Now, I can give my kids all of me. To want more out of life, it starts with becoming self-aware without judgement. Then you must act on a decision to change something about yourself. Turning to Jesus for help can lead you to miracles. He died on the cross for you and he's ready to give you a new life of freedom. Accepting him as your Lord and Savior truly does mean you are saved. Saved from punishment of sin and you are saved from yourself. Eventually, you will be called to go back home to God. Meanwhile you are here on earth to evolve into a spiritual being. Learning lessons as you go and to fulfill your life purpose. It is about keeping faith and staying focused. I am happy that Jesus led me to freedom, and I am forever grateful.

CHAPTER 5

THE POWER OF
THE MIND

Finally, the haunting of my past-memories were over, I overcame it. I felt amazing! Now, I needed to take charge of my mind. I was still learning about myself and the bad habits that needed to go. The question that I asked myself was, "how do I control my thoughts?" A human mind can have an average of sixty-thousand thoughts per day. To control your thoughts, first you need to know where they're coming from. Your beautiful soul that was given to you by God is the who you are, it's the psychological part of a person. Your thoughts come from your mind, which have an emotional side and an intellectual side. Your emotional side is your feelings and behaviors that form your personality. Your intellectual side is broken up into two consciousness. Your thoughts can come from your conscious mind and your subconscious mind. The conscious mind is being awake, aware, able to use logic, and communicate. Your thoughts can also come from your will or ego. It's the decision maker in you to choose or to reject something. Your subconscious mind is processing and managing information on what you see, hear and do. The subconscious mind will give you thoughts based on past and present experiences. If you've surrendered, then God is the decision maker and will communicate to you through your conscience and give you the best thoughts. Just when you think you understand your mind a bit there can be an outside force whispering in your ear. It's the devil. The devil is a fallen angel, he wanted full control and was kicked out of heaven by God. He whispers in your ear thoughts of defeat, fear, and of evil. Your thoughts come from seven different places, yikes. The good news is, when you surrender to God, your conscience is heightened, and your mind is renewed. Your conscience is a part of your personality. Basically, it serves as a moral compass in your heart to what's right and wrong. At some point I had so much going on in my mind, that inner chatter in my mind wouldn't shut up. I've asked God to help me decipher which thoughts to listen to. God, Jesus and the Holy Spirit bring peace with any thought or decision. This would need to be a daily choice for you to follow God's will and to renew your mind. The goal is to live in the moment with a renewed mind and only then you'll be able to control your thoughts. The Holy Spirit will protect you from thoughts that are not from love and bring you peace. God put his love in your heart and wants you to live a joyful life.

Surrendering your mind to God is giving up your way of thinking and to start thinking like him. You must get rid of your self-centered thinking. For years, I was following old programming and my ego created habits that were old too. These bad habits are changed through a renewal of the mind. Each day asking God for a renewal is asking for a new mind with power. We can't expect to automatically start thinking how God thinks. He's perfect. However, a part of the renewal process is to get rid of your old negative thoughts and put on God's thoughts. The overall purpose of having a renewed mind is to see things how God sees things. We are able to overcome any obstacles, if we have God's perspective. God's perspective is knowing that the outcome will favor you. When you have faith and keep the faith, God will then favor you. My advice is as soon as you wake up in the morning, say a prayer. A prayer of thankfulness and ask for a renewed mind. Pray throughout your day. Before bed add another thankfulness prayer. We're all already blessed, no need to ask God to bless us. A grateful heart will bring more to be grateful for. Stay focused on what you're thinking about. Did you know, that you can renew your mind by reading God's word? Find a bible version that suits you. Deciding to want a renewed mind shows your dedication towards God. We are all here on earth for a purpose and to live out that purpose for God.

"And be not fashioned according to this world: but be ye transformed by the renewing of your mind, that ye may prove what is the good and acceptable and perfect will of God." Romans 12:2 (American Standard Version)

Your mind can be a battlefield of unpleasant and pleasant thoughts. Your mind can get out of control, which will lead you to unfulfilling experiences. Outside forces can corrupt your mind, which will lead you to unfulfilling experiences too. The plan I have for you is a perfect plan. You already have everything you need, all you must do is realize it. Following my will, will give you traits of my character. The purpose for everyone is to think like me, act like me and love like me. Sharing my love to the broken hearted and the wounded. Ask for a renewed mind my child and you'll be able to live a life of wonder.

My mind, body and soul are healed but my mind needed my attention. Making the decision to change my ways of thinking, had opened new doors of possibilities. I believed I had God's power in me to create what I wanted, I just didn't know how to use it. I was thankful that I gave up my will and I was able to follow the Holy Spirit's guidance to my next learning experience. I could see the top of my mountain, but I had to keep going. God knew how to get me to my next level, leading me to books with the right information or giving me thoughts from his wonderful wisdom. God always had my best interest at heart. Finally, I bought my own bible and some other materials to read. My goals were to stay living in the moment and take control of my mind. Many thoughts would come to me, and sometimes I didn't even want to think anymore. I had a lot of contradicting thoughts going on. Positive thoughts and negative thoughts all at the same time. Thinking things like, "it's so hard for me to lose weight but I will get the weight off." In that sentence, I was acknowledging that losing weight was "so hard", so it would be difficult. At the same time, I will get the "weight off" was affirming I would lose the weight. So, I set myself up for a long weight loss journey. I'm glad I was paying attention to my conscience because I heard an amazing thought come to me which was, "the best way to get what you want is to affirm what you want. I am healthy, and my body works with me. My metabolism is a fat burning machine." Power is held in these conscious thoughts. Telling the universe that "I am healthy" and believing it, gives my body no choice but to create more good cells. The subconscious mind believes everything you tell it, so why not say what you are striving for.

Living in the moment took a lot of effort and discipline. I would pray daily to God to renew my mind and to help me control my thoughts. I learned to focus on my senses to keep me mindful. Every day I would practice on listening to my breathing, or I would feel my heartbeat. When I would eat, I asked myself, "how does the food taste?" Food taste so much better, when you pay attention. Another way to stay present was seeing natures beauty and smelling different flowers as I took walks. I started to realize that without effort, I would fall back into old habits. Losing weight was one of my goals. I watched what I said, ate and believed that I was going to lose weight. The results I created was thirty-three pounds of weight loss in six-months. Confidence in myself helped me stay focused on creating more for my life. There are many key components for manifestation. Being present of what you're saying and believing will help your desires to show up. The conscious mind is in charge and will always have the final say on what thoughts deserve to be your predominant thoughts. The predominant thoughts are the ones that you think about over and over in your conscious mind. Whether its negative or positive, your predominant thoughts will eventually manifest. Making time for self-development was a part of my daily life. I knew there was so much more to change about myself and I was ok with that. Pride couldn't get in my way; my focus was to keep Ruling My Life.

Another issue I had was having thoughts of complaints. Living in the moment had brought to my attention that I was a complainer. As soon as I woke up, I was complaining about how tired I felt, or my back hurting. Another complaint was believing a rainy day would ruin my whole day and living in Florida rain was frequent. Complaining continued, to complaining about not having enough money. Complaints, complaints and some more complaints. My family did a lot of complaining too. Sometimes, I would complain about their complaining. The vibe in the house felt heavy and everyone looked miserable. "What are we all miserable about?" The truth was we were miserable because we wanted to be. Our focus was on the wrong things, we displayed ungratefulness. I prayed to God to forgive me for being ungrateful. I asked him to help my family and I see the good in everything. A family meeting came about, and we had to be held responsible for our own actions. As the mother, I had to be the example for my kids. I decided to quickly put a stop to my complaining and started speaking life to my family throughout my day. Speaking words of praise to the Lord, words of gratitude and words of encouragement. As a family we built momentum and showed gratitude even for the little things, which was life changing. We were getting blessed with more income, more opportunities, and more wisdom. The house had a happier vibe, I could see smiles and hear laughter. My family and I showed a lot of love and gratitude towards each other too. If a complaint was said, the new focus was to ensure we did not stay complaining which would only allow a chain reaction of complaints to happen. Staying grateful and having a thankful heart puts a smile on Jesus face. He died to give us a good life and the least we can do is thank him. We thanked him for our new perspective and kicked out misery from our life. I can honestly say that now when I wake up, the first thing I say is, "thank you Jesus for this beautiful day, even if it's raining." With time, we learned to not complain but to make statements without having any emotion behind it. I believe when we speak with passion or emotion about anything, we will get more of it. Watching your emotions and staying grateful are more key components to help you manifest your desires.

Every morning, I would include more in my prayer to God. Thanking him was automatic, giving him praise for who he is and asking for a renewed mind. The battle was between my conscience, my conscious mind and my ego also known as my bad habits. One of these bad habits was my impatience while driving. One day while sitting in traffic, I began to get impatient. I was going back and forth in my mind if I should go on the median to cut off traffic. My conscious mind was saying, "no, there might be a cop." My conscience was telling me, "wait your turn." But my ego said, "you can do it!" So, I decided to go on the median, I was almost at the turning lane and my heart dropped. A cop on foot popped out of nowhere and flagged me down. It happened to be a sting operation in that area, three other cars got pulled over right after me. I was mad at myself because I listened to my ego. Sometimes, I thought situations would come my way as a test from God. Another example of my mind battles happened at the grocery store as I was putting my food in my car. In the past, when I was done with the cart, I would put the cart on the side and leave. This time around, my conscience told me, "put the cart back in the cart area." My ego tried to convince me to just leave it there, I was in a rush. My mood had changed, I started to feel annoyed and impatient. I took a moment to think and realized this was old bad habits. The right thing to do was, walk the cart to the cart area. As I was walking back to my car, my peace came back to me. As a Jesus believer, every day I must decide on who am I listening to. I'm learning to make decisions based on what's right and how I feel. If my peace is at stake, I'm not going that route. Listening to my conscience is one-hundred percent a peacekeeper and only good can come out of it. God has the best outcome for me, and I'll continue having a better relationship with him and myself.

Being aware of my conscious and subconscious occurred daily. One day it was a beautiful day out, I was on the road driving home and from one moment to the next I was sitting at a red light. I don't remember getting to this red light. "What just happened?" I thought. My subconscious mind drove, that's what happened. As I was driving, my conscious mind drifted away causing my subconscious mind to be in charge. Everything I've ever learned, including driving was stored in my subconscious mind. I'm grateful that I was able to drive safely. Over thinking things had allowed my conscious mind to not be present. On another day, I caught myself in deep thought while washing dishes. My conscious mind had drifted again. When my mind got back to reality, the dishes were just about done. I had an attitude and didn't know why. Praying about this was the only thing I could do. Taking charge of my conscious mind was my number one goal. I had to get rid of my bad habits of overthinking. I felt an urgency to learn about my subconscious mind. Wanting answers required action, it was that time again. I went to the library and the Holy Spirit led me to the precise aisle, shelf, row and book. I would feel chills throughout my body as I held the book I needed to read. What I've learned is as a child, what we see, hear and do is stored in our subconscious mind giving us a sense of direction of how our life will be experienced. Memories and life experiences shape our thinking patterns, beliefs and behaviors. As we get older, long-lived thoughts can create an attitude problem. It's crucial as parents to protect our children's innocence and fill their lives with positive programming. In doing that, it will create a leader. A leader who knows who they are, and they'll live a healthy marvelous life. Living in a dysfunctional upbringing will create negative programming; creating unnecessary struggles, low self-esteem and living a not so healthy life. My problem was, I had self-limiting thoughts. Second guessing myself because deep down inside I believed I wasn't good enough still. This old negative programming created bad habits that were on my radar to correct as soon as possible. Any child that lives with negative programming, needs to recover from their childhood at some point in their life. I pray for all the children; may they receive only positive programming as they are being raised.

Some more time went by, I felt like I was trapped in a web. The old negative programming was deeper than I thought. I wasted a lot of time living with the same thought process, attitudes and behavior. At least I knew what wasn't working for me anymore. My beliefs of "I'm not good enough" or "life is rough" had to stay in the web without me. I knew God was there to help me and I needed him to renew my mind again. Each time it was renewed, Jesus was my focal point. Praying to God for more confidence because I needed help correcting my thinking patterns. My conscience spoke to me and I listened. What I needed was to replace old beliefs, attitudes and behaviors with new beliefs, attitudes and behaviors. Intentionally I needed to interrupt my old thinking pattern by seeing, hearing and doing new things. I understood to freely live life in the moment it required time, discipline and patience with myself. On purpose I would do the opposite of everything, staying away from routine. Making confident decisions and expecting only good to come out of it, brought a new vibe to my world. Believing in myself gave me momentum for more positive change. I realized I was worthy of all the goodness life had to offer. I give God the glory for pointing me to the right direction. Listening to him has helped me get clarity on who I was and who I'm becoming. I believe I'm becoming the best version of myself and I'm excited about my growth. I'm thankful God will continue to guide me to anything and everything I need. Just remember, living in the moment works powerfully with your conscious thinking.

I believe when you're on the righteous path, the devil will focus on you more. He will plot, and whisper lies into your ears. His goal is to sow pride, doubt, division, temptation, fear and whatever it takes to turn people away from God. The devil was kicked out of heaven because he turned away from hearing God's voice and wanted to seek his own will. As humans, we turn away from hearing God's voice too and that's a sin that God doesn't forgive. Following your own will is technically a sin. The devil convinces us to use our human abilities to bring us under his control. The good news is we can resist him. When we take God's word seriously and listen to what he's asking for, only then is when we can resist the devil. We become untouchable! The devil tried tempting Jesus too. *"Again, the devil taketh him unto an exceeding high mountain, and showeth him all the kingdoms of the world, and the glory of them; and he said unto him, All these things will I give thee, if thou wilt fall down and worship me. Then saith Jesus unto him, Get thee hence, Satan: for it is written, Thou shalt worship the Lord thy God, and him only shalt thou serve. Then the devil leaveth him; and behold, angels came and ministered unto him." Matthew 4:8-11 (American Standard Version)* I never liked acknowledging that the devil had any type of influence in my life. The truth is, I've been tempted by the devil for decades. I know I allowed him to put negative thoughts in my mind. He's convinced me, he put seeds of fear and doubt in my mind. If you've ever felt fear, it's the devils work. Feeling fear is not from God. The devil wants to keep us from growing spiritually. He might be the ruler of the world, but he doesn't rule my life today. Being obedient and having confidence in who you are in Christ pours blessing over your life.

Cartoons and shows have depicted that we have a good angel and a devil on our shoulders. "Who do we listen too?" God created a perfect communication system for us. Our conscience is worth listening to because it's filled with God's goodness. We have a built-in indicator inside us to determine what's right and what's wrong. Just because our conscience is built-in, that doesn't mean we are connected and listening to it. If you are not saved, your ego is corrupted and will keep you from hearing God. If you ignore God for a long period of time, it will be hard for you to hear him. Lying, hypocrisy, and self-seeking ways will cause destruction to your conscience. There are many ways to connect or reconnect to your conscience. Praying to God for help and being still can restore your attention in hearing him again. What he wants from us is honesty, love and faithfulness. Clearing your conscience and confessing your sins will turn up your awareness so you can hear him. Surrendering everything to him is another way to hear him. Start loving yourself enough to give up your will and start following God's perfect will. Listening to your conscience is receiving God's wisdom. When I chose to listen to my ego, lessons were learned. When I chose to listen to my conscience, my love for God was displayed. My personal goal in life is to stay focused on listening to my conscience because I need my peace to stay. We're far from being perfect, but God gave us plenty of help for us to do our best.

Taking charge of your mind is an everyday choice you must make. Your thoughts control how you feel and what you allow into your life. You can think negative and feel sad, mad, self-pity, and depressed. You can think positive and feel happy, content, empowered, and blissful. What you think and feel about the most, will eventually show up in your life. Whether it's good or bad, it will come to you. That's why it's crucial that you stay living in the moment and pay attention to what you're thinking about. The quality of your life can depend on the quality of your thoughts. Your thoughts hold a vibration, energy or a frequency, all these words mean the same thing. God has given you his power to create and to line up your energy with the energy of the universe. God is the universe! The universe is filled with space, time and pure energy. In prayer, you can go to God directly and ask for anything. You can also use your thoughts to create anything you want. Either way, you must believe that God hears you and he'll give you what you're asking for. He allows you to start the request and he decides if you'll receive it or not, he's the finisher. You want good news, great breaks and awesome things in your life, you can have it all. You're deserving of it because God loves you.

The time has come to get clear about, "What do YOU want?" Make a list of your desires. Feel good about your list and start imagining that you already have it. Human thoughts are energy, a very powerful source that connects to the universe. The universe will then match your specific type of energy that you send out, and in return the universe gives you what you're thinking and feeling. God designed it that way. I've realized that even when I experienced bad breaks or problems, I had created that. My thoughts and feelings were negative, and the universe matched that vibe. Living in the moment, has helped me tremendously to stay on a positive vibration and to create wonderful things. Focusing, believing and feeling good about your desires will speed up the process of manifestation. "How will my desires come into my life?" God is the conductor of the universe, he's in charge, it's not your duty to figure out the "how." The "how" and the timing of it is in God's hands and believing in him is what matters most. Staying mindful and listening to your conscience is a serious reminder. You can't create greatness any other way. *"Ask, and it shall be given you; seek, and ye shall find; knock, and it shall be opened unto you." Matthew 7:7 (American Standard Version)*

Knowing things was one thing and applying what I learned was another. With God's help, I seized the moment to accept responsibility of my adulthood. The fact that I had created every experience with my thoughts and feelings, left me with an empowering feeling of, I can create. I'm now able to create new experiences and embrace all the beauty that life has to offer. What has helped me to believe that I can create, is having a renewed mind. A renewed mind brings a new perspective that anything is possible. Plus, I feel good about life, life is easy and

I'm worthy to receive abundance. I started with little things like a parking spot. I visualized myself getting the first spot closest to the store. Sure enough, I had manifested that parking spot. Smiling and giving God a thank you showed my appreciation to him. Some may call that a coincidence, but I call it creating my day. Practice makes perfect and in time I was manifesting bigger and better things. Life is not all about material stuff, but it sure feels good. You can create your day too. Learn to command your thoughts to do what you want. Build up a new belief system and have fun with it. Stay present, stay grateful, stay confident, stay hopeful and believe that your life can flourish. I love myself enough to want more out of life. I pray for what I need and for what I want, and I never limit God. I pray in advance too. "Lord, thank you for my tomorrow", shows faith. There is power in prayer and power in your thoughts, just believe. Depending on God for everything is the only way to go. God gets the glory for my healed mind, body and soul. God filled me up with his conviction, power and love. My long journey consisted of wanting change and fighting change. Self-awareness led me to make up my mind to Rule My Life. God opened doors to help me grow spiritually. He led me to Jesus healings, and I received a new life. Jesus saved me, gave me the Holy Spirit, awakened me, renewed my mind and transformed me. The Holy Spirit led the way on my teachings, from learning about myself to reading educational books and especially to the main book, the bible. I stand grateful feeling amazing that I never gave up on my spiritual journey and reached the top of my mountain. I made it, I am complete, I am free but not alone for I know that God is with me, God is the wind.

CHAPTER 6

GOD, JESUS AND THE HOLY SPIRIT

Do you want to Rule Your Life? If yes, you must act on a decision to change something about yourself or about a situation for a more meaningful life. That can mean getting rid of the old you and creating a new you. Letting go of your old ways will be the best decision you'll ever make. If your answer is no, I understand. For some reason the word "work" or "change" can put us in a paralyzed state. We allow doubt to kick in and fill us with lots of fear. Whatever is familiar to us can seem better than the unknown but result of change is unknown until we do it. It takes will power to get unstuck. The thought of change can make us afraid but what I've learned is, staying the same is the biggest thing to be afraid of. Some of the hardest parts to face on a self-journey of are learning the truths about yourself and putting in the self-help work to become a new better you. Decide that you're ready for change and put action behind that decision. Calling on God will make your journey less stressful. He knows what's best for you. He loves you. Everyone's destiny is to receive some type of healing and for you to live a life with freedom in your heart. The purpose of sharing my mistakes with you, is to help you save time and to learn by what not to do. I did it with baby steps, surrendered a little here and a little there. After I surrendered everything and accepted Jesus, my life was never the same. My faith in God gave me a bright path to follow. I became hungry for a deeper understanding on who my father in heaven is. Reading the stories in the bible heightened my imagination. I visualized all the magnificent things Jesus did for everyone. My love for Jesus grew too. I've built a relationship with him, I talk to him throughout my day. I'm able to live my life with confidence and know that I'm a living testimony to this world. Jesus is freedom and he saved my life. I'm able to live a better life now because of God. Are you ready to surrender everything? If yes, find a quiet place to relax your mind, body and soul. Read the "Meditation and Prayer Section." (The meaning of "Surrender Everything to God" is in the beginning of Chapter 3). If you're ready to do a partial surrender, go to the "Meditation and Prayer Section". You can do your own prayer and give God what you want. If your answer is no, skip the "Meditation and Prayer Section" and the "Release and Rebuke Section".

MEDITATION AND PRAYER SECTION

Take in a deep breath - God is the air you are breathing. Breathe out.

Surrender Meditation:

Breathe in - Allow yourself to receive my Holy Spirit. Breathe out.

Breathe in - Allow my spirit and love to fill you up. Breathe out - hurt and pain.

Breathe in - Allow yourself to feel the intense feeling of bliss. Breathe out - anger.

Breathe in - Peace. Breathe out - all sorrow.

You may be weeping. Let it out my child, it's my perfect timing for you. Be willing to let it all go.

Forgiveness Prayer: Father I am willing to forgive _____ for _____, I give this to you, help me to let go and forgive. I repent of my sins, thank you for forgiving me. In Jesus name, Amen.

Surrender Prayer: Father, I'm ready for a total surrender. I give you everything about me. I give you my mind, body and soul. Take my negative thoughts, my emotional pain, and my will. I'm ready to receive a renewed mind, your spirit, and your will. I accept Jesus Christ as my Lord and Savior. I believe Jesus died to save me from my sins and rose from the dead. Through faith in you, I have eternal life. In Jesus name, Amen.

> ***You have received my will and my spirit. Receive my healing power for your mind, body and soul. You are born again. I give you my peace.***

Did you feel the Holy Spirit's presence and peace? If yes, that is your confirmation that you've surrendered and accepted Jesus Christ as your Lord and Savior. I'm happy for you. If you were able to then skip the "Release and Rebuke Section". If you didn't feel the Holy Spirit's presence and peace, there might be a block. Read on to the "Release and Rebuke Section".

RELEASE AND REBUKE SECTION

If you are not receiving my spirit, there is a disconnect. All you need is a little faith. Holding on to unforgiveness is a sin or there might be evil present. You can pray.

Release and Rebuke Prayer: Father, I release all doubt I have, may my faith in you grow. I want to trust you, and may our spirits connect as one. I rebuke any evil that may be blocking our oneness. Evil must flee from me, my family and my surroundings. In Jesus name, Amen.

Try the "Meditation and Prayer Section" again, letting go of unforgiveness is a must. Allow the electric feeling of the Holy Spirit to flow through your body. Invite him in. Trust and believe God is here to help you.

"He healeth the broken in heart, And bindeth up their wounds." Psalm 147:3 (American Standard Version)

My hope is that you did a full surrender. If you did, how do you feel? A new life in Christ will bring you help, hope, peace, joy, healings and many teachings to follow. Embrace the change and changes to come. A part of you died when you accepted Jesus and you were filled with the Holy Spirit. God is gentle,

God is love and he will show you different things that will need fine tuning. Results don't come overnight either. Each day brings fresh starts and opportunities to change yourself, embrace that change. My advice to you is to include the following in your new life: Discover God's truth by spending time reading the word, find alone time to be with Jesus in prayer, worship him, listen to your conscience and obey him. The seeds you plant will produce the results you are looking for. You may also want to consider getting baptized soon, it's an act of faith and obedience to Jesus commands. Baptism declares that you're an overcomer because of Jesus. The best decision I made was surrendering, accepting Jesus and getting baptized. Receiving a renewed mind daily keeps my mind on the Lord. He hears my prayers and answers them too. I am adamant I will know our Father in heaven for I love him, and I am very grateful for Jesus' sacrifices. All the heaviness I was carrying is dead and gone. How amazing to know, that I have inherited a new life and I feel brand new. God's timing is on point, and you have inherited a new life too, by fully surrendering. Stay focused and continue to walk with God.

One day, I attended church and the band was playing Christian rock as their worship music. I began to worship Jesus. After a minute, I received a visual with my worship. Jesus and I were in the rock band and were jamming away on the guitar. My emotions were completely into it. The song was almost over, and the band started to play lightly. I felt an electric feeling on my shoulder. Someone had tapped me with their fingers. I opened my eyes and looked, there was no one to my left. I looked to my right and the person there was in worship still, standing away from me. The electric feeling tap was the Holy Spirit. I asked Jesus, "Lord, was it ok that I visualized you playing the guitar?" Instantly, I felt the Holy Spirit go through me, I could feel him from head to toe. I heard a gentle voice say, "I have humor too." At that moment, I felt like I was his best friend. Worship and prayer don't have to be uptight or follow certain rules. You can speak to Jesus from your heart, anywhere, at any time. Most of my prayers, I visualize Jesus and I on the beach. Whatever works, do it. Having a relationship with Jesus will bring guidance into your daily life. He wants you to follow him and know his voice. I've learned to put God first, then family and then business. When our life has balance, only goodness can come our way.

Sharing my testimonies with you, gives honor and glory to God. Years ago, I was pregnant with my son and had a migraine headache. I took two Tylenol pills and the migraine wouldn't go away. Getting on my knees to pray to Jesus for help was the smartest thing I did. After I prayed, I felt a tingling sensation on my head. It felt like two hands were holding my head and when the sensation stopped, my migraine was gone. I got up and said, "thank you Jesus!" I slept like a baby for a few hours and woke up fine. Another story I would like to share where prayer was the answer was a time when I was a passenger in a car. A family member was speeding and lost control of the car. We were headed towards a brick wall, I embraced myself for impact. In my head, I said, "Jesus help us!" Instantly, the car shifted to a different direction going between a tree and a light pole. We ended up in a dirt area and the car was spinning out of control. Finally, the car stopped. We were able to drive out of that area. I was grateful that we were ok, and I felt our angels helped us by taking over the wheel. The next day, I went back to the area where our lives could've ended. The tree and the pole weren't too far from each other. Miraculously, we fit through it just breaking the side mirror of the car. I believe God has given everyone guardian angels to help us daily. I know this just like I know the steering wheel was moved by our angels.

I yearned to see my angel, I became curious on how my angel looked. I prayed to Jesus to show me my angel. That same day, my daughter Camila saw an angel in our kitchen. I couldn't see it, but she saw it. She described the angel as feminine with dark hair. I took a picture and the image of the angel was captured! I thanked Jesus and my angel for saving our lives. Our whole life is a testimony. Each time we wake up in the morning, Jesus gave that to us. Each time we breath, Jesus gave that to us. Each time we hug our children, Jesus gave that to us. He gave us the opportunity to live our life, he just wants to be able to guide, restore and renew us.

Living your life for Jesus is a calling, a calling from heaven. You live out your destiny here on earth and eventually go back to Jesus and God the Father who is in heaven. A spiritual person knows that we are all one with God. You should consciously, honor God for your oneness and be grateful for him because you need him. If you attend church already, Amen. If you want to go to church, pray and God will lead you to one. Having a personal relationship with Jesus can happen anywhere. It doesn't mean you have to attend church daily. I stopped attending church regularly and that was a personal decision that I made. My home is my sanctuary, I feel the Holy Spirit's presence. Studying the word informs me of the truth I need to know. The Holy Spirit helps me accept the truth and being obedient helps me apply the truth. The purpose of living my life for Jesus is to change myself inside and out. God knows, we're far from being perfect, but we could build our character like Jesus. Each day, I allow the Holy Spirit to lead and if I'm veering off track, the Holy Spirit will speak to me through my conscience. My character has changed tremendously; I was a big gossiper, I would curse like a sailor and blame others for everything. I faced many truths that God revealed to me.

Living for Jesus is a forever thing, he consistently corrects me. I'm not bothered by it because my ego is tamed. When God convicts me, I ask for forgiveness immediately and grow from that experience. Through Jesus, I'm able to get rid of bad habits. My goal is to be more like Jesus, having his character is a work in progress. He was a perfect being and that is someone I'm willing to follow.

Reading and understanding the bible has shined a new light in my life. Find a version that you're comfortable with. I received a deep understanding of the old testament and the new testament. The truth is in God's word, his word expanded my thinking. It's at reach for anyone that wants to be spiritually free. We are free because of Christ's sacrifice but not free to do what we want. True freedom is becoming a slave to Christ. When we submit to Jesus all our sins lose power over us. Jesus power will take over and cleanse us. Following and trusting him creates a peace of mind and eliminates sinful habits. Jesus lived a selfless life by being focused on benefiting others. He had the desire to help and heal his brothers and sisters. While being on the cross he spoke to God with concern. ***"My God, my God, why hast thou forsaken me? Why art thou so far from helping me, and from the words of my groaning?" Psalm 22:1 (American Standard Version)*** God never abandoned Jesus. Jesus had no sins and our sins were given to him as his final sacrifice. He felt the separation from God and gave his last cry. He had disappeared from the presence of God because sin can't exist in God's presence. Jesus lived a perfect life for us, because we couldn't do it ourselves. I deserved to feel what he felt. He took on my sins and he chose to die for me. Receiving Jesus into my life brings me to my knees. I worship Jesus, he is my king. In prayer, I thank him for being my Savior. Sharing Jesus love by truly helping others is something I must do. Jesus takes care of me, he always has and always will. My everyday living is based on following the Holy Spirit's guidance and to share the love of Christ.

I can't believe years ago, I decided to hide my feelings and not deal with them this only caused me to stop loving myself. Lies were made up in my head, that I wasn't worthy of true happiness. I took many stops along the way, with a few derailed courses but I always found my way back. What I've learned throughout my spiritual journey is, self-awareness without judgement is important and you must start there. Deciding to change my life was a part of my purpose, so that I may fulfill my destiny. Getting rid of the old me was a part of God's plan, I'm glad I put my trust in him. Discovering God was the best thing for me, God is everything. He is love, power, understanding, faithfulness - all that is positive and great. I can honestly say because of him I feel lighter, confident, happy and I truly love myself. I'm grateful that my mind, body and soul were healed, and I have received victory. God gave me a burning desire to take care of myself. I became awakened, my mind was renewed, and I was transformed. The Holy Spirit's guidance led me to do self-help, which brought me to a place of reinvention. I reinvented who I was and I'm thankful for that day when I decided to Rule My Life. I'm standing on top of my mountain and I feel complete! I'm able to live again and embrace new experiences with peace. I understand who I am now because of God. Each day, I yearn to keep fulfilling my God given purpose and to keep growing spiritually. I decided to write this book to help others who are in the same boat that I was in. I want to share God's love by helping others. Also, I want to bring awareness to adults to protect their kids' innocence. I purchased a computer for the sole purpose of writing this book. I was excited about my project and the excitement fizzled away within a few days. I just played around with the computer and got familiar with it. After that, I placed it on a shelf. Sometimes, I would place things on top of the computer, out of sight out of my mind. I just wasn't ready to start. Months passed, I prayed for motivation because dust was starting to accumulate.

One morning, I had the Holy Spirit in me. Nothing could get in my way. My husband and my children were great distractions, but I went outside to my patio with a "Do Not Disturb" sign. Most of the **Bold** inspirational writing was written that day. Those words are from God. I typed with confidence and knew those words held power. Now, it was my turn to put my life on paper. The computer went back on the shelf for months. The "I'm not good enough" to write a book thought was in control. I wasn't ready to hear any criticism. Excuse after excuse, I was done with hearing the negative within myself. At this point in my life I knew better. I fixed my crown and just focused on God! I prayed, "Lord, forgive me for not having faith in myself or you. In Jesus name, Amen." An idea came to me, to write what I know. As I was writing, I cheered for my younger self for being strong and laughed at the young adult for being foolish. God gets the glory for my transformation and for the completion of this book. My purpose in writing this book, was to point the way to God, Jesus and the Holy Spirit for healing. I wrote this book in obedience and I know many will seek God now. Keep climbing your mountain, you will reach the top! God loves you.

I purposely put this paragraph twice in this book. I know some of you came to this last paragraph first, hoping to find your missing answers. I have a message for you. God is your answer. I wrote this book because I truly want to help you. God healed my life and he can heal yours too. God's power can heal your past and present traumas. Some of you may have had a good childhood but experienced trauma as an adult. Some of you may have the little girl or boy in you feeling trapped because of your trauma. I do understand that as a human we question, "why? Why did this have to happen to me?" Especially when things are done to us from a young age, when we are helpless and vulnerable. The memories of any trauma stay with you throughout life. You may think you can ignore or avoid the pain by choosing sex, drugs, and/or alcohol. How long do you live your counted days living in misery? God is waiting for you to stop fighting change and allow him to help you become free of those memories. Take back what's rightfully yours. Peace, love, freedom, healing and joy awaits. Right now, seize this moment and become self-aware because you are important. Decide to want more out of life and get ready to Rule Your Life. Then God will give you steps to take so you can receive your healings. It's important to start living again but it starts with a decision. Your decision can help you create a new experience, and a new you. You are the son or daughter of the Almighty God, fix your crown. Stand up straight and know that you are blessed already. Get excited about the day and allow yourself to become truly fulfilled. *"Now unto him that is able to do exceeding abundantly above all that we ask or think, according to the power that worketh in us, unto him be the glory in the church and in Christ Jesus unto all generations for ever and ever. Amen." Ephesians 3:20-21 (American Standard Version)*

Dear Reader,

I would like to thank you for your patronage of this book. I hope this book, "RULE YOUR LIFE" has made a positive impact on your life. I would love to hear all about it, you can email me at:

ruleyourlifenow@gmail.com

P.S. Life is good!

Thank you,
Author Jenica Lee

Bibliography

Public Domain Bible Version. (Copyright waived). American Standard Version. (ASV). Retrieved from www.biblegateway.com

4167942-00967631

Printed in the United States
By Bookmasters